LangGraph RAG

Building Smarter Multi-agent Systems with Knowledge Graphs and
Retrieval-Augmented Generation

James Wiglow

Copyright Page

Title: *LangGraph RAG: Building Smarter Multi-agent Systems with Knowledge Graphs and Retrieval-Augmented Generation*

Author: James Wiglow

Disclaimer:

The information in this book is provided "as is." The author and publisher make no warranties or representations with respect to the accuracy or completeness of the contents, and are not responsible for any errors or omissions in the content. The publisher does not assume any liability for any damage resulting from the use of the information in this book.

Table of Content

Chapter 1: Introduction: Unlocking the Power of Multi-agent Systems

In this chapter, we will introduce the concept of **multi-agent systems**, explore the role of **LangGraph** and **Retrieval-Augmented Generation (RAG)**, and explain why combining these two technologies is the key to building **smarter, more adaptable AI systems**. Let's begin by understanding the fundamentals.

1.1 What are Multi-agent Systems?

A **multi-agent system (MAS)** refers to a system where multiple **agents** interact with each other to achieve specific goals or solve problems. These agents can be simple or complex, depending on the tasks they are designed to perform. An **agent** in the context of AI is a software entity that acts autonomously or semi-autonomously to perform tasks. Each agent in a multi-agent system can make decisions, interact with other agents, and influence the environment in which it operates.

Key Features of Multi-agent Systems:

1. **Autonomy**: Agents have the ability to make decisions independently, without constant human intervention.
2. **Communication**: Agents interact with one another by exchanging information, either to collaborate or compete for resources.
3. **Cooperation**: In many systems, agents work together to solve a common problem, sharing information and resources to improve performance.
4. **Flexibility**: Agents can operate in dynamic environments and adapt to changing circumstances.

Example of a Multi-agent System:

Consider a **traffic management system** where multiple agents (each representing a traffic light) communicate with each other to optimize traffic flow in a city. Each agent observes traffic in its area and adjusts its signal to minimize congestion. The agents cooperate by sharing information such as the number of cars in different regions, optimizing the flow of traffic across the entire city. In this case, the agents work towards a common goal—reducing traffic congestion—while acting independently in their own regions.

Types of Multi-agent Systems:

- **Cooperative Systems**: All agents in the system work towards a common goal. An example is a **distributed sensor network** where sensors share data to monitor environmental changes like pollution or temperature.
- **Competitive Systems**: Agents in the system compete for limited resources, such as in **marketplaces** or **auction systems**.
- **Mixed Systems**: A combination of both cooperative and competitive elements. An example is a **robotic swarm**, where individual robots may compete for resources but cooperate to complete a task.

1.2 Introduction to LangGraph and RAG: How They Work Together

What is LangGraph?

LangGraph is a framework designed to help build intelligent systems using multi-agent architectures, where agents work in a coordinated manner to solve complex tasks. It combines **knowledge graphs, workflow management**, and **agent-based architectures** to allow seamless interaction between agents and external data sources.

LangGraph utilizes **graph-based structures** to model knowledge and relationships between different entities. These graphs represent how different agents interact with each other and how they access and process information. In LangGraph, each agent can be equipped with specific tasks, ranging from simple data retrieval to complex decision-making processes.

What is RAG (Retrieval-Augmented Generation)?

Retrieval-Augmented Generation (RAG) is a technique that enhances the **generation capabilities** of language models by incorporating real-time **data retrieval**. Instead of relying solely on pre-trained models and static data,

RAG systems dynamically retrieve information from external sources like **databases**, **APIs**, or **knowledge graphs** to augment the language model's output.

Here's how RAG works:

1. **Retrieval**: When a question or task is given to the system, the first step is to **retrieve relevant information** from a pre-defined knowledge base or external data source.
2. **Generation**: The retrieved data is then used to **augment the generative process** of the language model. This allows the system to generate more relevant and factually accurate responses based on up-to-date information.

How LangGraph and RAG Work Together

LangGraph and RAG complement each other by **enhancing the intelligence** and **relevance** of multi-agent systems. LangGraph's **agent-based architecture** and **knowledge graph** capabilities provide a solid framework for organizing and managing complex systems, while **RAG** enhances agents' ability to interact with **external knowledge sources**.

Let's take an example: Imagine a multi-agent system designed to help users find information on the internet. One agent is responsible for understanding the user's query, while another agent is responsible for retrieving relevant documents from the web. Using RAG, the retrieval agent can fetch up-to-date information from the internet and send it to the language model agent, which generates a coherent and relevant response to the user. LangGraph's agent framework ensures that the agents communicate and collaborate effectively to solve the problem.

By combining LangGraph's agent architecture with RAG's dynamic retrieval capabilities, we can build more **adaptive**, **reliable**, and **intelligent systems** that respond to real-world data in real-time.

1.3 Why LangGraph + RAG is the Future of Intelligent Systems

Smarter Decision-Making with Real-Time Data

The combination of **LangGraph's multi-agent system** and **RAG's dynamic retrieval capabilities** allows for real-time decision-making in **complex environments**. Traditional AI systems that rely solely on pre-trained models may struggle to adapt to new information or changing circumstances. However, with RAG, LangGraph agents can access and incorporate real-time data, which allows them to make more **informed**, **accurate decisions**.

Increased Efficiency and Collaboration

LangGraph's multi-agent architecture allows for specialized agents to handle different tasks within a larger system. RAG enhances these agents' ability to access and utilize external data, making the system as a whole more **efficient**. Instead of relying on a single large model, LangGraph breaks down tasks into smaller, manageable components, each handled by an agent. RAG ensures that these agents can retrieve the most relevant data for their specific tasks.

Scalability

LangGraph provides a scalable framework where agents can be added or removed based on the needs of the system. As the system grows, the agents can independently handle more complex or diverse tasks, making it ideal for large-scale deployments. RAG ensures that as the system scales, each agent can continue to retrieve and use the most relevant data without needing constant retraining.

Adaptability to New Domains

Combining LangGraph and RAG allows systems to be more **adaptive** to new domains. As new data becomes available, agents can dynamically retrieve and incorporate it into their decision-making processes. This makes the system **domain-agnostic**, meaning it can be applied to a wide range of industries without requiring a complete redesign.

1.4 Real-World Applications of Multi-agent Systems

Multi-agent systems are already making a significant impact across a variety of industries. Let's explore a few real-world applications:

1.4.1 Autonomous Vehicles

In **autonomous vehicles**, multi-agent systems help manage the coordination between the car, sensors, and other vehicles on the road. Each vehicle can be an **agent**, interacting with others to prevent collisions, optimize traffic flow, and ensure safety. LangGraph can be used to model the interactions between these vehicles, while RAG can help retrieve real-time traffic information from external sources.

1.4.2 Smart Grids

In **smart grid systems**, multiple agents can be responsible for managing electricity distribution, ensuring that power is allocated efficiently and that outages are detected and resolved quickly. LangGraph can help coordinate these agents, while RAG can provide up-to-date data on electricity demand and weather patterns to optimize energy distribution.

1.4.3 Healthcare Decision Support

In **healthcare**, multi-agent systems are used to support decision-making by analyzing patient data and recommending treatment options. Each agent may specialize in a different aspect of healthcare, such as diagnostics, treatment plans, or medication management. LangGraph can help coordinate these agents, while RAG can fetch the latest medical research to inform decision-making.

1.4.4 Financial Systems

In **financial markets**, multi-agent systems help with real-time trading, risk assessment, and portfolio management. Each agent can be responsible for tracking different assets or strategies. RAG enhances the system by retrieving the latest market data, allowing agents to make more informed investment decisions.

1.5 Key Insights

- **Multi-agent systems** involve multiple agents that collaborate or compete to achieve a common goal or solve a problem.
- **LangGraph** provides a framework for designing and managing multi-agent systems, utilizing **knowledge graphs** and agent-based interactions to model complex workflows.
- **RAG** enhances multi-agent systems by retrieving real-time data from external sources and incorporating it into the decision-making process, making systems smarter and more adaptive.
- **LangGraph + RAG** represents the future of **intelligent systems**, enabling real-time, informed decision-making, and scalable, adaptable AI systems.
- **Real-world applications** of multi-agent systems include **autonomous vehicles**, **smart grids**, **healthcare**, and **financial systems**, showcasing their versatility and impact across industries.

In summary, **multi-agent systems** powered by **LangGraph** and **RAG** offer significant advantages in building **intelligent, adaptive, and scalable AI solutions**. By utilizing **specialized agents, knowledge graphs**, and **real-time data retrieval**, these systems can solve complex problems more efficiently than traditional approaches. As we progress through this book, we will explore how to build and optimize such systems, leveraging the power of LangGraph and RAG for real-world applications.

Chapter 2: The Fundamentals of LangGraph

In this chapter, we will dive into the **architecture of LangGraph**, its **key concepts**, and its **building blocks**. We will explore how LangGraph is structured to facilitate communication and collaboration between agents in a multi-agent system. By the end of the chapter, you will have a clear understanding of the fundamental components of LangGraph and how to create a simple agent workflow.

2.1 LangGraph Architecture: Components and Structure

Overview of LangGraph Architecture

LangGraph is designed as a framework to build intelligent systems using **multi-agent architectures**. The architecture is **modular**, enabling easy integration of various components and functionality based on the system's needs. The core components of LangGraph are:

1. **Agents**: These are the primary building blocks of LangGraph. Each agent has specific tasks or responsibilities and interacts with other agents to achieve a collective goal.
2. **Knowledge Graphs**: A graph-based structure where data is organized in nodes and edges. The nodes represent entities, and the edges define relationships between them. Knowledge graphs serve as a data structure for representing the system's domain knowledge.
3. **Communication Layer**: The agents communicate with each other through a predefined communication protocol. This layer handles data exchange, decision-making, and coordination between agents.
4. **Workflows**: LangGraph uses workflows to define the sequence of tasks or operations agents perform. Workflows determine the order in which agents execute their tasks and how they collaborate.
5. **External Data Sources**: LangGraph agents can also integrate with external data sources such as APIs, databases, or real-time data feeds to retrieve or update knowledge.

6. **Control Logic**: This component governs how agents interact with each other, making decisions based on predefined rules or dynamic inputs from the environment.

LangGraph System Design

LangGraph systems are generally **distributed**, where agents perform specific roles and share information with other agents to solve a larger problem. Each agent is responsible for a set of tasks and can access or update information within the knowledge graph.

For example, in an **autonomous traffic management system**, different agents might control different intersections, and they must coordinate with each other to optimize traffic flow across the entire city. Knowledge graphs store the traffic data, such as traffic patterns and vehicle counts, which the agents can access in real time. Communication between agents allows them to make informed decisions, such as adjusting traffic light timings based on real-time traffic conditions.

LangGraph's Core Architecture:

- **Agent 1 (Traffic Light at Intersection A)**:
    - Responsibilities: Monitor traffic, adjust traffic light timings based on conditions at the intersection.
    - Communication: Sends traffic data to Agent 2 (nearby intersection).
- **Agent 2 (Traffic Light at Intersection B)**:
    - Responsibilities: Adjust traffic light timings based on information from Agent 1, manage congestion at its own intersection.
    - Communication: Receives data from Agent 1 and shares its own data with Agent 3.
- **Knowledge Graph**:
    - Nodes: Represent various intersections, vehicle counts, traffic signals, and their states.
    - Edges: Define relationships such as traffic flow between intersections, signal timings, and traffic density.

2.2 Key Concepts: Agents, Knowledge Graphs, and Workflows

Agents

An **agent** in LangGraph is an autonomous or semi-autonomous entity responsible for executing tasks, collecting data, or making decisions within a system. Agents are typically designed to:

- Perform **specific tasks** in the system.
- Interact with **other agents** and **external data sources** to complete their tasks.
- **Collaborate** with other agents to solve larger problems.

For instance, in a **customer service** system, one agent may be responsible for greeting customers, while another agent handles inquiries and yet another resolves complaints. These agents communicate and cooperate to ensure efficient service delivery.

Knowledge Graphs

A **knowledge graph** is a data structure used to represent information about the world in a graph format. In LangGraph, knowledge graphs allow agents to represent their **domain knowledge** in a structured manner. Each node represents an **entity** (e.g., a customer, product, or service), and the edges represent relationships between these entities.

For example, in an **e-commerce system**, a knowledge graph could represent products, customers, and the interactions between them (e.g., "Customer A purchased Product B"). This structure allows agents to efficiently query and reason about the relationships and facts stored in the graph.

Workflows

A **workflow** is a set of tasks or activities performed by agents in a defined order. Workflows can be simple, where tasks are executed sequentially, or more complex, involving multiple agents and parallel tasks.

For instance, in a **logistics system**, the workflow might involve agents that:

- **Track incoming shipments**.
- **Route products to different warehouses**.
- **Schedule deliveries to customers**.

LangGraph allows workflows to be dynamic, meaning agents can adapt to changing circumstances. For example, if a shipment is delayed, the workflow can be adjusted to reroute it through an alternative path.

2.3 Building Blocks of LangGraph: How Agents Communicate

In a **multi-agent system**, effective communication is essential for cooperation and task completion. LangGraph supports **asynchronous communication** where agents can share information, request data, or make decisions based on the actions of other agents.

Communication in LangGraph:

1. **Messages**: Agents communicate by sending and receiving **messages** that contain data or commands. Messages can be used for:
   - **Sharing data** (e.g., traffic conditions, inventory levels).
   - **Requesting information** (e.g., "What is the status of the traffic at Intersection A?").
   - **Directives or commands** (e.g., "Change the light timing to 30 seconds at Intersection A").
2. **Message Types**:
   - **Query Messages**: Sent when one agent needs information from another (e.g., "What is the current stock level of Product X?").
   - **Command Messages**: Sent to instruct another agent to perform a task (e.g., "Schedule a delivery for Customer Y").
   - **Informational Messages**: Sent to update other agents on current states (e.g., "Traffic is congested at Intersection A").
3. **Communication Protocol**: LangGraph agents follow a **standardized protocol** to ensure messages are understood and processed correctly. Protocols define how messages are structured, how agents respond to requests, and how failures are handled.

Agent Interaction Example:

In a **warehouse management system**, two agents might communicate as follows:

- **Agent 1 (Inventory Monitor)**: "Query Message" – "What is the stock level of Product X?"
- **Agent 2 (Stock Controller)**: "Informational Message" – "Product X has 50 units in stock."
- **Agent 1**: "Command Message" – "Reorder Product X when stock level drops below 10 units."

2.4 Mini-Project: Building a Simple Agent Workflow in LangGraph

In this mini-project, we will build a simple **multi-agent workflow** using LangGraph. Let's consider a **task assignment system** where agents work together to complete a project. Each agent will handle one task in the workflow and communicate with other agents to ensure tasks are completed in the correct sequence.

Step 1: Define the Agents

We will create three agents:

- **Agent 1**: Handles task creation.
- **Agent 2**: Manages task assignment.
- **Agent 3**: Executes tasks.

Step 2: Define the Workflow

- **Agent 1** creates a task and sends a message to **Agent 2** for assignment.
- **Agent 2** assigns the task to **Agent 3**.
- **Agent 3** executes the task and reports back to **Agent 1** that the task is complete.

Step 3: Implement the Agents and Communication

Let's write a Python example using a basic structure for these agents.

```python
class Agent1:
    def create_task(self):
        task = "Task: Complete the report"
        print(f"Agent 1: Created {task}")
        # Send task to Agent 2 for assignment
        agent2.assign_task(task)

class Agent2:
    def assign_task(self, task):
        print(f"Agent 2: Assigning {task} to Agent 3")
        # Send task to Agent 3 for execution
        agent3.execute_task(task)

class Agent3:
    def execute_task(self, task):
        print(f"Agent 3: Executing {task}")
        # Task completed
        agent1.task_complete(task)

class Agent1:
    def task_complete(self, task):
        print(f"Agent 1: Task '{task}' completed.")

# Initialize agents
agent1 = Agent1()
agent2 = Agent2()
agent3 = Agent3()

# Start the workflow
agent1.create_task()
```

Step 4: Running the Workflow

When you run this program, you will see the agents work together to complete the task. The output will be:

```
Agent 1: Created Task: Complete the report
Agent 2: Assigning Task: Complete the report to Agent 3
Agent 3: Executing Task: Complete the report
Agent 1: Task 'Task: Complete the report' completed.
```

This mini-project demonstrates how **agents communicate** and how workflows are **structured** in LangGraph.

2.5 Key Insights

- **LangGraph** provides a modular framework for building multi-agent systems, with agents communicating and collaborating to achieve shared goals.
- **Agents** in LangGraph are responsible for specific tasks, and the **knowledge graph** stores and organizes the data they use to make decisions.
- **Workflows** are essential for determining how agents interact with each other and the order of task execution.
- **Communication** between agents is crucial and is handled through standardized message types like **queries**, **commands**, and **informational messages**.

2.6 Reflection: How can you use LangGraph to model a real-world task?

Now that you understand the basic components of LangGraph, think about how you could apply this framework to a real-world problem. Consider the following questions:

- What real-world system could benefit from a **multi-agent approach**?
- How would you structure the **

agents** and **workflow** in that system?

- What **knowledge** do the agents need, and how will they share information with each other?
- How can LangGraph's **communication layer** be used to ensure efficient interaction between agents in your system?

Take time to reflect on these questions and consider how LangGraph can be applied to improve decision-making, task management, and collaboration in real-world scenarios.

In this chapter, we've covered the **fundamentals of LangGraph**, including its **architecture**, key **concepts** like agents and workflows, and how agents communicate within the system. Through the mini-project, you've gained practical experience in building a simple agent workflow. With these foundational concepts, you're now ready to explore more complex systems and applications in the following chapters.

Chapter 3: Understanding RAG (Retrieval-Augmented Generation)

In this chapter, we will introduce **Retrieval-Augmented Generation (RAG)**, a powerful technique that enhances traditional language models by combining them with external data retrieval mechanisms. We will explore how RAG works, how it can be integrated into **LangGraph** for smarter agents, and how to implement a basic RAG retrieval system within LangGraph.

3.1 What is RAG and How Does It Enhance Language Models?

Introduction to RAG (Retrieval-Augmented Generation)

Retrieval-Augmented Generation (RAG) is an advanced method that improves the performance of language models by **retrieving external information** before generating text. Traditional language models rely solely on their pre-trained knowledge to generate responses, which means they may struggle with providing up-to-date or specific information. RAG solves this problem by **augmenting** the model's generation process with real-time, relevant data retrieved from external sources, such as databases, APIs, or knowledge graphs.

Key Features of RAG:

1. **Data Retrieval**: Before generating a response, the system retrieves relevant information from an external knowledge base (e.g., documents, search engines, databases).
2. **Text Generation**: The retrieved data is then passed to the language model to **augment** its output, resulting in a more accurate, relevant, and factually correct response.
3. **Enhanced Context**: RAG allows the language model to draw from external data, which helps it provide more detailed and up-to-date answers than a standard model relying solely on its training data.

How RAG Enhances Language Models

Traditional language models like GPT or BERT rely on their **training data** to generate responses, which means they can't answer questions about things they haven't been trained on. RAG overcomes this limitation by **integrating real-time data** into the process, allowing models to retrieve and incorporate new information as needed. This makes RAG systems particularly useful for tasks that require **up-to-date knowledge**, such as customer support, research, or any domain where information is constantly changing.

3.2 How RAG Works: Data Retrieval and Augmentation Process

The process of **data retrieval and augmentation** in RAG involves two main stages:

1. **Data Retrieval**:
   - When a query or prompt is received, the **retrieval mechanism** first searches an external knowledge base for relevant information. This can include:
     - **Documents**: Text files, articles, or reports.
     - **APIs**: External data sources that provide real-time information (e.g., news feeds, stock prices).
     - **Databases**: Structured data from databases or knowledge graphs.
   - The retrieval system selects the most relevant pieces of information based on the query.
2. **Data Augmentation and Generation**:
   - The retrieved data is then passed to the language model, which uses this information to **augment** the generation process. The model generates a response based on both the query and the augmented data.
   - For instance, if the query asks for a stock price, the model might retrieve real-time stock data and generate a response like, "As of 2:00 PM, the stock price of XYZ company is $150."

Example of the RAG Process:

1. **Query**: "What is the latest stock price of Company XYZ?"
2. **Retrieval**: The system queries an external API or knowledge base for the latest stock price of Company XYZ.
3. **Augmentation**: The retrieved data (stock price) is then fed into the language model.
4. **Generation**: The model generates the final response: "The current stock price of Company XYZ is $150, up 3% from yesterday."

This process allows the model to answer specific queries with **real-time, accurate information** instead of relying on the static knowledge encoded during training.

3.3 Integrating RAG with LangGraph for Smarter Agents

Integrating **RAG** into LangGraph can make multi-agent systems more **dynamic** and **adaptive**. LangGraph's agent architecture is well-suited for incorporating RAG's data retrieval and augmentation capabilities. By allowing agents to retrieve relevant information from external sources, you enable them to **generate smarter, context-aware responses**.

How RAG Integration Enhances LangGraph Agents:

1. **Real-Time Data Access**: LangGraph agents can retrieve data from live sources (e.g., APIs, databases) and incorporate this into their decision-making processes.
2. **Improved Decision-Making**: Agents can use real-time data to **make more informed decisions**. For example, a **financial agent** could use RAG to fetch the latest market data and adjust its investment strategies accordingly.
3. **Dynamic Workflows**: With RAG, agents in LangGraph can adapt their workflows based on the latest data. For example, a **logistics agent** could retrieve current traffic data to reroute deliveries in real-time, improving efficiency.

Example of LangGraph with RAG:

Let's say we have a **multi-agent traffic management system** in LangGraph, where one agent manages traffic lights, and another agent monitors traffic flow. By integrating RAG:

- The **traffic light agent** could use real-time traffic data from external sources (e.g., cameras, sensors, or traffic reports) to optimize its signal timings.
- The **traffic monitoring agent** could use RAG to retrieve up-to-date weather data or accident reports to adjust traffic flow predictions.

In this system, RAG enhances the decision-making capabilities of the agents, making them more adaptive and efficient.

3.4 Mini-Project: Implementing a Basic RAG Retrieval System in LangGraph

Now that you understand the core principles of RAG and its integration with LangGraph, let's implement a **basic RAG retrieval system** in LangGraph. In this mini-project, we will create a simple agent workflow where one agent retrieves information from an external knowledge source, and another agent generates a response based on that information.

Step 1: Define the Agents

We will create two agents:

- **Agent 1 (Data Retriever)**: Responsible for retrieving data from an external source (e.g., an API or a knowledge base).
- **Agent 2 (Response Generator)**: Uses the retrieved data to generate a response.

Step 2: Set Up the Workflow

We'll simulate a **news retrieval system** where Agent 1 retrieves the latest news headlines and Agent 2 generates a response based on those headlines.

Step 3: Implement the Code

```python
import requests

class Agent1:
    def retrieve_data(self):
        # Simulate retrieving news from an external source
        url = "https://api.example.com/latest-news"
        response = requests.get(url)
        data = response.json()  # Assuming the API returns
JSON data
        print("Agent 1: Retrieved data from external source")
        return data['headlines']  # Example field in the data

class Agent2:
    def generate_response(self, data):
        # Generate a response based on the retrieved data
        print("Agent 2: Generating response based on
retrieved data")
        response = f"Here are the latest news headlines: {',
'.join(data)}"
        return response

# Initialize agents
agent1 = Agent1()
agent2 = Agent2()

# Step 1: Retrieve data from the external source
retrieved_data = agent1.retrieve_data()

# Step 2: Generate a response using the retrieved data
response = agent2.generate_response(retrieved_data)
print(response)
```

Step 4: Explanation of the Code

- **Agent1 (Data Retriever)**: This agent simulates retrieving the latest news from an external API. It makes an HTTP request to a hypothetical news API and returns the headlines.
- **Agent2 (Response Generator)**: This agent receives the retrieved data (the news headlines) and generates a response, summarizing the latest headlines.

Step 5: Running the Mini-Project

When you run this project, you would see output similar to this (assuming the API response is structured correctly):

```
Agent 1: Retrieved data from external source
Agent 2: Generating response based on retrieved data
Here are the latest news headlines: "Market hits all-time
high", "Weather forecast predicts rain tomorrow", "New tech
gadget released"
```

3.5 Key Insights

- **RAG** enhances traditional language models by allowing them to retrieve and incorporate **real-time data** into their generation process.
- The process consists of **data retrieval** from external sources, followed by **augmentation** where the language model uses the retrieved data to generate more accurate and context-aware responses.
- **LangGraph integration** with RAG allows for dynamic, real-time data retrieval and decision-making, improving agent collaboration and adaptability in multi-agent systems.
- RAG is particularly useful in scenarios requiring **up-to-date knowledge** or access to external databases or APIs.

3.6 Reflection: In what scenarios does RAG enhance language model performance?

Consider the following questions to help you reflect on where RAG might enhance the performance of a language model:

- **Dynamic Information**: In situations where knowledge is constantly evolving (e.g., news, stock prices, weather), how does RAG improve a language model's ability to provide **relevant and accurate** responses?
- **Specialized Knowledge**: How can RAG help when the model needs to retrieve **specialized knowledge** from an external database (e.g., medical data, scientific research)?
- **Real-time Context**: How does RAG's ability to pull real-time information enhance decision-making in a **real-world application**, such as in autonomous vehicles or personalized marketing systems?

Reflecting on these scenarios will help you better understand how RAG can **enhance language model performance** in various contexts.

In this chapter, we explored **Retrieval-Augmented Generation (RAG)** and how it enhances language models by enabling them to incorporate real-time data into their responses. We also discussed how RAG can be integrated with **LangGraph** to create smarter, more adaptable agents. Finally, the mini-project demonstrated how you can implement a simple RAG retrieval system in LangGraph. With this understanding, you are now equipped to leverage RAG to build more powerful, dynamic AI systems.

Chapter 4: Building Blocks of LangGraph Systems

In this chapter, we will explore the foundational components of LangGraph systems, including **agents**, **knowledge graphs**, and **workflows**. Understanding these core building blocks is crucial to effectively utilizing LangGraph to create intelligent, collaborative, and adaptive multi-agent systems. We will also provide an **interactive example** of how to set up agents and knowledge graphs in LangGraph, helping you apply these concepts practically.

4.1 Designing and Managing Agents in LangGraph

What is an Agent in LangGraph?

In LangGraph, an **agent** is an autonomous entity that performs tasks, makes decisions, and communicates with other agents to accomplish goals within a multi-agent system. Each agent in LangGraph is **task-specific**, meaning it is designed to handle a particular part of the overall system, but agents can **collaborate** and **coordinate** with one another to achieve more complex objectives.

Agent Characteristics in LangGraph:

1. **Autonomy**: Agents can function independently, making decisions based on predefined rules or data. They do not require constant human oversight.
2. **Communication**: Agents exchange information with other agents or external systems to complete their tasks. Communication can be **asynchronous** (where agents send messages and act later) or **synchronous** (where agents interact in real-time).
3. **Task Execution**: Each agent is assigned specific tasks or responsibilities. It may execute simple actions, like querying a database, or complex tasks, like controlling a traffic system or responding to customer queries.

4. **Adaptability**: Agents in LangGraph can adjust their behavior based on the data they receive. They can react to changes in their environment or workflow by recalculating actions or altering their strategies.

Agent Design in LangGraph

Designing agents in LangGraph typically involves:

- **Task Definition**: Specify the agent's responsibilities within the system.
- **Knowledge Integration**: Equip agents with access to **knowledge graphs** or other external data sources to help them make informed decisions.
- **Communication**: Define how agents will send messages to each other and external systems.
- **Behavioral Rules**: Set rules for how agents will behave in different situations (e.g., when to retrieve data, when to adjust task priorities).

Example of Agent Design:

Imagine you are designing an **order fulfillment agent** in an e-commerce system:

- The **order fulfillment agent** could be responsible for checking stock levels and coordinating the shipping process.
- It would communicate with the **inventory agent** to check stock levels and with the **shipping agent** to schedule deliveries.
- The agent would adjust its behavior based on real-time stock data, querying a knowledge graph to ensure it only processes orders for available items.

Managing Agent Behavior

Once designed, **agent management** in LangGraph involves:

- **Agent Initialization**: Setting up agents when the system starts, configuring their tasks and capabilities.
- **Task Scheduling**: Organizing and scheduling tasks so that agents can execute them in an efficient order.

- **Agent Termination**: Managing how agents terminate or shut down their tasks when no longer needed, ensuring that resources are freed up.

4.2 Understanding Knowledge Graphs: What They Are and How They Function

What is a Knowledge Graph?

A **knowledge graph** is a **structured data representation** that connects entities (nodes) with relationships (edges) to form a graph. Each node in the graph represents an entity (e.g., a person, product, or event), and each edge represents a relationship between those entities (e.g., "Person X is a customer of Company Y"). Knowledge graphs allow for **efficient storage** and **retrieval** of complex, interconnected data, making them ideal for scenarios where relationships between data points are key to understanding or solving a problem.

Components of a Knowledge Graph:

1. **Entities (Nodes)**: Represent objects or concepts. For example, in a **social network knowledge graph**, entities could include **people, groups**, and **posts**.
2. **Relationships (Edges)**: Define how entities are related. For example, **Person A** "likes" **Post X**, or **Person B** "is friends with" **Person A**.
3. **Attributes**: Entities and relationships can have attributes (e.g., **Person A** might have attributes like **name, age**, and **location**).

How Knowledge Graphs Work

A knowledge graph supports **complex queries** by providing a flexible structure for accessing and reasoning about data. Instead of simply storing data in rows and columns, knowledge graphs represent **relationships** between entities, which allows for more sophisticated **searches** and **insights**.

For instance, in a **movie recommendation system**, a knowledge graph could represent movies, genres, and user ratings. By analyzing the relationships between these entities (e.g., "User A liked Action movies"), the system can generate personalized recommendations.

Applications of Knowledge Graphs in LangGraph:

- **Data Storage**: Store entities and their relationships to create a dynamic, flexible data model.
- **Efficient Queries**: Retrieve data based on relationships rather than just searching for individual entities.
- **Enhanced Reasoning**: Use knowledge graphs to make inferences about data (e.g., if two users are connected through a shared interest, they might be interested in similar products).

4.3 Managing Agent Workflows and Tasks: Coordination and Collaboration

What are Workflows in LangGraph?

In LangGraph, a **workflow** refers to the series of tasks or actions that agents must perform in a specific order. Workflows define how tasks are **coordinated** between multiple agents and how they **collaborate** to achieve a goal. Each agent in the system is responsible for performing a specific task, and workflows ensure that these tasks are executed in the correct sequence.

Key Aspects of Agent Workflows:

1. **Task Scheduling**: Determining the order in which tasks should be executed.
2. **Agent Interaction**: Agents communicate and coordinate with each other, passing information and triggering tasks.
3. **Error Handling**: If an agent encounters an issue (e.g., an inability to retrieve data), workflows should include contingency steps to ensure the task can still be completed.
4. **Parallelization**: Some workflows may involve multiple agents working in parallel to complete tasks simultaneously, which can improve efficiency.

Example of an Agent Workflow:

In a **customer service system**, the workflow might involve:

- **Agent 1 (Inquiry Agent)** receives a customer query.
- **Agent 2 (Database Agent)** retrieves relevant information from the knowledge base.
- **Agent 3 (Response Agent)** generates and delivers a response to the customer.

Each agent in this workflow performs its task at the right time, and they cooperate to ensure that the customer's query is handled efficiently.

Managing Task Dependencies and Deadlocks:

LangGraph allows you to manage **task dependencies** (i.e., some tasks cannot proceed without others being completed first) and avoid **deadlocks** (where tasks are stuck in an unresolvable state).

4.4 Interactive Example: Setting Up Knowledge Graphs and Agents in LangGraph

Now let's set up a simple knowledge graph and agent workflow in LangGraph, where we build a small **task management system** that retrieves information from a knowledge graph and processes it through agents.

Step 1: Define the Knowledge Graph

Let's create a basic knowledge graph representing a **project management system**. The graph will have nodes for **tasks**, **employees**, and **projects**, and edges representing relationships such as "Assigned To" and "Part Of".

```
import networkx as nx

# Create a directed graph (for task flow)
project_graph = nx.Graph()

# Add nodes (tasks, employees, projects)
project_graph.add_node("Task 1", type="task",
status="pending")
project_graph.add_node("Employee A", type="employee",
role="developer")
```

```
project_graph.add_node("Project Alpha", type="project",
deadline="2023-12-31")

# Add relationships (edges)
project_graph.add_edge("Task 1", "Employee A",
relation="Assigned To")
project_graph.add_edge("Task 1", "Project Alpha",
relation="Part Of")

# Visualize the graph (if using in a Jupyter notebook or
similar environment)
print(project_graph.nodes(data=True))
print(project_graph.edges(data=True))
```

Step 2: Define the Agents

Let's define two simple agents:

- **Agent 1 (Task Manager)**: Responsible for assigning tasks.
- **Agent 2 (Status Checker)**: Responsible for checking the status of tasks.

```
class TaskManager:
    def assign_task(self, task, employee):
        print(f"Task '{task}' assigned to Employee
'{employee}'")

class StatusChecker:
    def check_task_status(self, task):
        status = project_graph.nodes[task]["status"]
        print(f"The status of {task} is: {status}")

# Initialize agents
task_manager = TaskManager()
status_checker = StatusChecker()

# Step 3: Workflow: Assign task and check status
task_manager.assign_task("Task 1", "Employee A")
status_checker.check_task_status("Task 1")
```

Step 3: Running the Workflow

When the system runs, it will output:

```
Task 'Task 1' assigned to Employee 'Employee A'
The status of Task 1 is: pending
```

Step 4: Explanation

In this interactive example:

- We set up a **knowledge graph** representing tasks, employees, and projects.
- We defined **two agents**: one for assigning tasks and one for checking the task status.
- The agents collaborate, using the knowledge graph to **retrieve** and **update** task data.

4.5 Key Insights

- **Agents** in LangGraph are autonomous entities that perform tasks, make decisions, and communicate with other agents.
- **Knowledge Graphs** represent entities and their relationships in a graph format, facilitating efficient data retrieval and reasoning.
- **Workflows** define the sequence of tasks and ensure that agents collaborate and coordinate to achieve a common goal.
- LangGraph's **flexible architecture** allows you to build complex, adaptive multi-agent systems by integrating agents, knowledge graphs, and workflows.

4.6 Reflection: How would you design an agent to query and update a knowledge graph in real-time?

Reflect on the following questions as you consider designing a real-time agent system:

- What specific tasks would you assign to the agent? For example, would it be tasked with **querying data** or **updating information** within the knowledge graph?
- How would you handle real-time updates to ensure that the agent has access to **up-to-date information**?

- What kind of **queries** would the agent need to run on the knowledge graph (e.g., retrieving the status of a project, listing available employees, etc.)?
- How would the agent handle **multiple simultaneous requests** or data conflicts?

By thinking through these considerations, you will better understand how to integrate agents and knowledge graphs to create dynamic, real-time systems.

This chapter has provided a deep dive into **LangGraph's core components**: **agents**, **knowledge graphs**, and **workflows**. You now have a solid understanding of how to design and manage agents, how knowledge graphs work, and how to use LangGraph's architecture to build effective multi-agent systems.

Chapter 5: Deep Dive into Knowledge Graphs

In this chapter, we will explore **Knowledge Graphs** in depth, covering how to build, populate, and query them efficiently. Knowledge graphs are powerful tools for representing data and relationships in a structured, graph-based format. We will also dive into a **mini-project** that allows you to create and query a knowledge graph for an AI task. By the end of the chapter, you will have a clear understanding of how to work with knowledge graphs in LangGraph systems and how to optimize them for efficiency.

5.1 Building Knowledge Graphs: Tools and Techniques

What is a Knowledge Graph?

A **knowledge graph** is a type of graph where **nodes** represent entities (such as people, places, products, or concepts) and **edges** represent the relationships between those entities (e.g., "is a friend of", "is located in", "has product type"). Knowledge graphs allow you to model complex, interconnected data and provide a way to efficiently query relationships.

Tools for Building Knowledge Graphs

There are several tools and libraries available for building knowledge graphs. Some of the most popular include:

1. **Neo4j**:
    - Neo4j is one of the most popular **graph databases**. It allows you to store, query, and manage large knowledge graphs. Neo4j supports the **Cypher query language**, which is designed specifically for graph databases.
2. **NetworkX**:
    - **NetworkX** is a Python library used for the creation, manipulation, and study of complex networks. It can be used for **building graphs** where nodes and edges represent

relationships. While it's not as powerful as a dedicated graph database like Neo4j, it's great for building small to medium-sized knowledge graphs.

3. **RDF (Resource Description Framework)**:
   - o RDF is a standard for representing graph-based data. It's used extensively in the **semantic web** for representing relationships between entities. Tools like **Apache Jena** or **RDFLib** can be used to build and manage RDF-based knowledge graphs.

4. **Apache TinkerPop**:
   - o TinkerPop is an open-source graph computing framework that provides a set of standard interfaces for interacting with graph databases. **Gremlin**, the query language of TinkerPop, allows you to express queries for navigating and manipulating graph data.

5. **OWL (Web Ontology Language)**:
   - o OWL is a semantic web language used to define ontologies that describe the types of objects and relationships in a knowledge graph. It's used for more **formal and complex models** of knowledge.

Building Knowledge Graphs with NetworkX

NetworkX can be used to create a simple knowledge graph. Here's an example of how to use it to model a basic set of relationships:

```python
import networkx as nx

# Create an empty graph
G = nx.Graph()

# Add nodes (entities)
G.add_node("John", type="Person")
G.add_node("Mary", type="Person")
G.add_node("Book A", type="Book")

# Add edges (relationships)
G.add_edge("John", "Mary", relationship="friend")
G.add_edge("John", "Book A", relationship="author_of")

# Display nodes and edges
print("Nodes:", G.nodes(data=True))
print("Edges:", G.edges(data=True))

# Access relationship
```

```
for u, v, data in G.edges(data=True):
    print(f"{u} is {data['relationship']} with {v}")
```

Output:

```
Nodes: [('John', {'type': 'Person'}), ('Mary', {'type':
'Person'}), ('Book A', {'type': 'Book'})]
Edges: [('John', 'Mary', {'relationship': 'friend'}),
('John', 'Book A', {'relationship': 'author_of'})]
John is friend with Mary
John is author_of with Book A
```

Best Practices for Building Knowledge Graphs:

- **Start with clear definitions** of entities and relationships: Define what types of entities (e.g., people, products, locations) and relationships (e.g., "works at", "lives in") will be in the knowledge graph.
- **Consistency in labeling**: Ensure that entities and relationships are labeled consistently to avoid confusion and errors.
- **Use efficient data structures**: For large graphs, consider using graph databases (e.g., Neo4j) to efficiently store and query the graph.
- **Design with scalability in mind**: As the graph grows, ensure that it can scale to handle large amounts of data.

5.2 Populating Knowledge Graphs with Real-World Data

Once you've designed the structure of your knowledge graph, the next step is to **populate** it with real-world data. Data can be pulled from various sources, including:

- **APIs**: Real-time data sources like news, weather, and financial data.
- **Databases**: Structured data in relational databases or NoSQL databases.
- **Web Scraping**: Extracting information from web pages using tools like **BeautifulSoup** or **Scrapy**.
- **Manual Entry**: Sometimes, data is entered manually into a graph, especially when it's a new graph or the data is not readily available.

Populating a Knowledge Graph with External Data

In this example, we will simulate populating a knowledge graph with data about **movies** and **actors** from an external source, such as a CSV file:

```python
import pandas as pd

# Example CSV data: Movies and their actors
data = {
    "Movie": ["Movie A", "Movie B", "Movie C"],
    "Actor": ["John Doe", "Jane Smith", "John Doe"],
}

# Convert to DataFrame
df = pd.DataFrame(data)

# Create a new graph
movie_graph = nx.Graph()

# Add nodes and relationships from CSV data
for _, row in df.iterrows():
    movie_graph.add_node(row["Movie"], type="Movie")
    movie_graph.add_node(row["Actor"], type="Actor")
    movie_graph.add_edge(row["Movie"], row["Actor"],
relationship="acted_in")

# Display the knowledge graph
print("Nodes:", movie_graph.nodes(data=True))
print("Edges:", movie_graph.edges(data=True))
```

Output:

```
Nodes: [('Movie A', {'type': 'Movie'}), ('Movie B', {'type':
'Movie'}), ('Movie C', {'type': 'Movie'}),
        ('John Doe', {'type': 'Actor'}), ('Jane Smith',
{'type': 'Actor'})]
Edges: [('Movie A', 'John Doe', {'relationship':
'acted_in'}),
        ('Movie B', 'Jane Smith', {'relationship':
'acted_in'}),
        ('Movie C', 'John Doe', {'relationship':
'acted_in'})]
```

Techniques for Populating Knowledge Graphs:

- **Data Ingestion**: Use scripts or APIs to **automate data entry** into the graph.

- **Data Cleaning**: Ensure that the data entered into the graph is **clean** and consistent, handling missing data or invalid entries.
- **Real-time Updates**: For dynamic knowledge graphs, set up **automated processes** to pull in new data or update the graph regularly.

5.3 Querying Knowledge Graphs for Efficient Retrieval

How to Query a Knowledge Graph

Once the graph is populated with data, the next step is to **query** the graph for specific information. Querying a knowledge graph involves searching for nodes, edges, and their relationships based on certain criteria.

For instance, if you want to find all actors who acted in a particular movie, you can **query the graph** like this:

```
# Query: Find all actors who acted in "Movie A"
actors_in_movie_a = [neighbor for neighbor in
movie_graph["Movie A"] if movie_graph["Movie
A"][neighbor]["relationship"] == "acted_in"]
print(f"Actors in Movie A: {actors_in_movie_a}")
```

Output:

```
Actors in Movie A: ['John Doe']
```

Optimizing Queries for Large-Scale Graphs

As the graph grows larger, it is important to optimize queries to ensure **fast retrieval** of data. Some techniques to achieve this include:

- **Indexing**: Create indexes on frequently queried entities (e.g., movie names, actor names).
- **Graph Partitioning**: Divide the graph into smaller, more manageable subgraphs to speed up queries.
- **Caching**: Cache commonly requested data to avoid repeated queries to external databases or APIs.

Common Query Types:

- **Node Search**: Find a node based on a specific property.
- **Edge Search**: Retrieve all relationships between nodes.
- **Pattern Matching**: Find nodes or relationships that match a particular pattern (e.g., "Actors who acted in a movie that John Doe also acted in").

5.4 Mini-Project: Creating and Querying a Knowledge Graph for an AI Task

In this mini-project, we will create a simple **AI knowledge graph** that models **products** and their **attributes**. We will then query the graph to find products that meet certain criteria.

Step 1: Define the Knowledge Graph

Let's build a graph where products are nodes and their attributes (e.g., price, category) are stored as properties on the nodes.

```python
# Define a product knowledge graph
product_graph = nx.Graph()

# Add products as nodes
product_graph.add_node("Laptop", price=1000,
category="Electronics")
product_graph.add_node("Phone", price=500,
category="Electronics")
product_graph.add_node("Table", price=150,
category="Furniture")

# Query: Find all products in the Electronics category
electronics = [node for node, data in
product_graph.nodes(data=True) if data["category"] ==
"Electronics"]
print(f"Electronics products: {electronics}")
```

Step 2: Explanation

This graph has three products, each with a **price** and **category** attribute. We then query the graph to find all products in the **"Electronics"** category.

Step 3: Running the Mini-Project

Running the project will output:

```
Electronics products: ['Laptop', 'Phone']
```

**

5.5 Key Insights**

- **Knowledge graphs** represent data as a set of interconnected entities and relationships, enabling more complex and flexible data retrieval.
- Tools like **NetworkX**, **Neo4j**, and **RDF** can be used to build and manage knowledge graphs, while **APIs**, **databases**, and **web scraping** can be used to populate them with real-world data.
- **Efficient querying** of knowledge graphs is essential for fast data retrieval, especially in large-scale applications.
- **Optimization techniques** such as indexing, partitioning, and caching can significantly improve query performance.

5.6 Reflection: How would you optimize a knowledge graph for fast retrieval in large-scale applications?

Reflect on the following questions to consider optimization techniques:

- How would you handle **large amounts of data** in a knowledge graph to maintain fast retrieval times?
- What methods would you use to ensure **efficient storage** and **querying** for a knowledge graph with millions of entities?
- How would you design the **query architecture** to prioritize speed without sacrificing accuracy?

By reflecting on these questions, you can better understand how to scale knowledge graphs for large-scale applications.

This chapter has provided a deep dive into **building**, **populating**, and **querying knowledge graphs**. We've also demonstrated how to create a knowledge graph and query it for an AI task, giving you a solid foundation for using knowledge graphs in LangGraph systems.

Chapter 6: How RAG Works: The Inner Mechanics

In this chapter, we will explore the inner workings of **Retrieval-Augmented Generation (RAG)**. We will break down its architecture, understand the processes behind data retrieval and augmentation, and examine advanced techniques for improving retrieval efficiency. Furthermore, we will discuss how to **optimize RAG for LangGraph** systems to ensure effective augmentation and provide a challenge to implement a custom retrieval-augmented pipeline. By the end of this chapter, you will have a deep understanding of the mechanics of RAG and how it fits into LangGraph systems.

6.1 RAG Architecture: Components and Process

Overview of RAG Architecture

Retrieval-Augmented Generation (RAG) is a hybrid approach that combines two key components:

1. **Retrieval System**: This component is responsible for fetching relevant data from external sources, such as a knowledge base, database, or external API.
2. **Generation Model**: This is a pre-trained **language model** (such as GPT or BERT) that generates responses based on both the user's query and the external data retrieved by the retrieval system.

The general architecture of a RAG system consists of the following steps:

1. **Query Reception**: The system receives a query or input text, which needs to be answered or processed.
2. **Data Retrieval**:
   o The system searches an **external knowledge base** or API to retrieve relevant documents or information that can help answer the query.

o The retrieval mechanism typically involves searching through a set of documents or entries based on keywords, embeddings, or other search techniques.

3. **Augmentation**:
   o Once the relevant data is retrieved, it is passed to the **language generation model**, which augments its output using the external data.
   o The generation model produces a response or output by combining the context of the original query with the retrieved data.

4. **Response Generation**: The final response is generated, incorporating both the query and the augmented external information, and sent back to the user.

Key Components of RAG:

- **Retrieval Engine**: This part of the system searches for relevant information from a pre-defined knowledge base, such as a database or external API.
- **Language Model (LM)**: This model generates the output based on the retrieved data. Common LMs include Transformer-based models like GPT, T5, or BERT.
- **Augmentation**: The model is augmented with the additional data retrieved from the knowledge source, which enriches the generated response.

How RAG Works in Practice:

Consider an example where the query is about the latest news on a particular topic:

- The **query** might be: "What's the latest news about renewable energy?"
- The **retrieval system** fetches the most recent articles related to renewable energy from an external database or news API.
- The **language model** then combines the fetched information with the original query and generates a detailed response that includes the latest news, facts, and details.

Visualizing the RAG Process:

1. **Input**: "What is the status of renewable energy in 2023?"
2. **Retrieval**: The system retrieves documents or data from news articles, scientific papers, or databases.
3. **Generation**: The model augments the query using the retrieved data and generates a response.
4. **Output**: "Renewable energy saw significant growth in 2023, with a 15% increase in solar energy generation globally..."

6.2 Advanced Techniques for Data Retrieval (e.g., vector search, API integration)

Vector Search

One of the most advanced techniques for improving **data retrieval** in RAG systems is **vector search**. Vector search involves representing both the query and documents in a **high-dimensional vector space**. Each piece of data (query and documents) is embedded into a vector, which captures its semantic meaning rather than relying on exact keyword matches.

- **How it works**:
    - Use **embeddings** (e.g., **word embeddings, sentence embeddings**) to represent textual data as vectors in a high-dimensional space.
    - During the retrieval phase, the system calculates the similarity between the query vector and document vectors, selecting the documents with the highest similarity scores.
- **Advantages**:
    - **Semantic Search**: It allows for more **accurate retrieval**, even when the query doesn't exactly match the document text.
    - **Handling Synonyms**: Vector search can match queries and documents that use different terminology but have similar meanings.
- **Example:**
    - Query: "What's the latest on solar power?"
    - Retrieved documents might include articles using different words like "photovoltaic energy" or "solar panel technology" but are still relevant.

API Integration

For real-time data, integrating external **APIs** into the RAG pipeline can significantly improve the accuracy and relevance of the retrieved information.

- **How it works**:
  - The retrieval system calls an API, such as a weather service, stock market feed, or news aggregator, to pull in up-to-date information.
  - The retrieved data is then passed to the language model, which augments its generation with this real-time information.
- **Example**:
  - Query: "What is the current stock price of Company XYZ?"
  - The system calls a stock price API (e.g., Alpha Vantage, Yahoo Finance), retrieves the latest price, and augments the response with that data.

Combining Vector Search with API Integration

By combining **vector search** with **API integration**, you can build more powerful RAG systems that not only retrieve semantically similar documents but also access live data that enhances the system's ability to respond to real-time queries.

6.3 Optimizing RAG for LangGraph: Ensuring Effective Augmentation

Optimizing Retrieval for Efficiency

In LangGraph, the integration of RAG systems can be optimized by ensuring that data retrieval is as efficient as possible. Here are some strategies:

1. **Caching**: Cache frequently accessed data to reduce the time spent querying external sources.

o For example, if a certain set of news articles or financial data is frequently retrieved, cache the data for quick access rather than querying the same external API repeatedly.
2. **Indexing**: Use indexing techniques to make retrieval faster. Implement **inverse indexing** or **embedding-based indexes** to quickly find relevant documents.
3. **Parallel Retrieval**: For large-scale systems, enable parallel retrieval, where the system fetches multiple pieces of data at once, ensuring faster response times.
4. **Filtering**: Before performing a retrieval, filter the dataset to only include relevant data. This reduces the scope of the search and speeds up the process.

Optimizing Generation for Accuracy

Once the retrieval phase is optimized, the next step is to enhance the **generation** part of the RAG system:

1. **Contextual Augmentation**: Ensure that the retrieved data is **relevant** to the original query. This can be achieved by **filtering** the data based on its relevance or by using more **specific embeddings** for certain domains (e.g., medical, finance).
2. **Fine-tuning the Language Model**: Fine-tune the pre-trained model on your specific domain, so it better understands how to combine retrieved data with the query for more **coherent responses**.

Example of Optimizing RAG in LangGraph:

In LangGraph, agents can use RAG to access real-time information and augment their decision-making process. For example:

- **Traffic Agent**: Fetches traffic data via an API and combines this with a historical knowledge graph to optimize routing decisions.
- **Customer Service Agent**: Retrieves customer data from a CRM system and augments the response with external product information to provide personalized answers.

By ensuring that both the retrieval and generation components are optimized, LangGraph agents can respond faster and more accurately.

6.4 Challenge: Implementing a Custom Retrieval-Augmented Pipeline for LangGraph

Challenge Objective:

Create a custom RAG pipeline in LangGraph that integrates real-time data retrieval, such as news articles, and uses that data to augment the agent's response to a query.

Step 1: Define the Query and Data Retrieval

We will use a **news API** to retrieve the latest articles on a specific topic. The agent will fetch the articles and use them to generate a detailed response.

```python
import requests

# Define the news API
API_KEY = "your_news_api_key"
URL = f"https://newsapi.org/v2/everything?q=renewable
energy&apiKey={API_KEY}"

def fetch_news():
    response = requests.get(URL)
    data = response.json()
    articles = data['articles']
    return [article['title'] for article in articles]

# Retrieve the news articles
news_data = fetch_news()
print(news_data)
```

Step 2: Integrate with LangGraph Agent

Next, we will create an agent in LangGraph that retrieves the news and generates a response by combining the retrieved articles with a pre-trained language model.

```python
class RAGAgent:
    def __init__(self, news_data):
        self.news_data = news_data

    def generate_response(self, query):
        # Augment the query with the latest news
        augmented_query = f"{query} Here are the latest
updates: {', '.join(self.news_data)}"
```

```
        return f"Response: {augmented_query}"

# Instantiate the agent and generate a response
rag_agent = RAGAgent(news_data)
response = rag_agent.generate_response("Tell me about the
latest trends in renewable energy")
print(response)
```

Step 3: Explanation

- The agent retrieves news articles using an external API.
- It then generates a response by combining the query with the retrieved data.
- The final output will be a **dynamic response** that is augmented with real-time information.

Step 4: Running the Challenge

Running the code will output a response such as:

```
Response: Tell me about the latest trends in renewable
energy. Here are the latest updates: "Solar energy
advancements in 2023", "Global wind power growth in Q1", "New
policies for renewable energy investments"
```

6.5 Key Insights

- **RAG** enhances language models by integrating external data into the generation process, making the responses more accurate and up-to-date.
- The architecture of RAG involves two key components: **data retrieval** and **generation**. By retrieving relevant data and combining it with the model's generation process, RAG ensures more contextualized responses.
- Techniques like **vector search**, **API integration**, and **caching** can improve both **data retrieval efficiency** and **generation accuracy**.
- In LangGraph, **optimizing RAG** involves improving both the retrieval and generation stages to ensure effective augmentation for agents.

6.6 Reflection: What are the trade-offs between real-time data retrieval and model accuracy in RAG systems?

Consider the following when reflecting on the trade-offs:

- **Real-time Data Retrieval**: While retrieving real-time data can make the system more accurate by providing the latest information, it can also increase **latency** (delay in fetching the data). How might this impact user experience?
- **Model Accuracy**: Fine-tuned models are more accurate in specific domains, but they may not have access to

the latest data. How do you balance the need for a **real-time response** with the accuracy of **pre-trained models**?

By thinking through these trade-offs, you will be better equipped to design **effective RAG systems** that provide fast, accurate, and relevant information.

In this chapter, we explored how **RAG works**, the **components** involved, and how to optimize the system for effective data retrieval and augmentation. The **challenge** allowed you to implement a simple custom RAG pipeline, integrating external data into a LangGraph agent's decision-making process. With this knowledge, you can enhance your RAG systems to deliver more accurate, real-time responses.

Chapter 7: Integrating LangGraph and RAG for Powerful Systems

In this chapter, we will focus on how to integrate **LangGraph** with **Retrieval-Augmented Generation (RAG)** to create **powerful, adaptive systems**. We will discuss how LangGraph agents can use RAG for **real-time data retrieval**, explore best practices for integrating the two technologies, and address common **integration challenges**. Additionally, we will walk through an **interactive learning example** where we will integrate LangGraph agents with an external knowledge base to enhance their decision-making capabilities.

7.1 How LangGraph Agents Use RAG for Real-Time Data Retrieval

The Role of LangGraph Agents in RAG

LangGraph agents are autonomous entities within a **multi-agent system** that perform specific tasks, make decisions, and interact with other agents. When combined with **Retrieval-Augmented Generation (RAG)**, these agents can enhance their decision-making capabilities by **retrieving real-time data** from external sources before generating responses.

In the **LangGraph + RAG** integration:

1. **Agents retrieve** data from external knowledge bases, APIs, or databases.
2. **RAG augments** the agents' responses by using the retrieved data to generate more accurate, up-to-date information.
3. The system allows the agent to **dynamically adapt** to changing conditions in real-time, making it ideal for use cases like customer service, autonomous vehicles, and real-time analytics.

How Data Retrieval Enhances LangGraph Agents:

Consider the example of an **e-commerce agent** that provides product recommendations. When the agent receives a customer query like, "What are the latest reviews for product X?", it would:

1. **Use RAG** to query a review API or a database for the most recent reviews.
2. **Augment the response** by combining the retrieved review data with the agent's pre-trained model, ensuring the response is relevant and up-to-date.

The integration of RAG enables the agent to not only rely on its internal knowledge but also to pull in real-time data from external sources, enhancing the quality and relevance of the generated responses.

Example Workflow for LangGraph Agent Using RAG:

- **Query**: "What are the latest stock prices of renewable energy companies?"
- **Data Retrieval**: The agent queries a stock price API for real-time data.
- **RAG Augmentation**: The agent combines the retrieved stock price data with a pre-trained language model to provide a detailed response: "The stock price of XYZ Energy has increased by 4% today, and the overall market trend for renewable energy is positive."

By integrating RAG with LangGraph agents, you enable them to adapt their behavior dynamically based on real-time data, improving both the accuracy and relevance of their actions.

7.2 Best Practices for Integrating LangGraph with RAG

1. Efficient Data Retrieval:

- **Caching**: Cache frequently retrieved data to reduce the number of API calls or queries to external systems. This ensures that agents can respond quickly, especially in high-demand scenarios.
- **Indexing**: Use indexes for your knowledge base or external data sources to ensure faster retrieval of relevant information. Techniques like **embedding-based indexing** or **inverted indexes** can significantly improve retrieval performance.

2. Ensuring Data Relevance:

- **Contextual Retrieval**: Make sure the data retrieval process is **context-aware**. For instance, when an agent queries for external data, it should filter out irrelevant or outdated information. Use filtering mechanisms such as **keyword matching**, **semantic search**, or **vector search** to ensure the data is highly relevant to the query.
- **Pre-processing Data**: Before passing the data to the language model for augmentation, pre-process the data to ensure it is in a format the model can easily consume. For example, remove unnecessary text, reformat data, or ensure data consistency.

3. Seamless Integration:

- **Modular Architecture**: Design your LangGraph agents to work in a **modular** fashion, so that adding or removing RAG components (like different data sources) does not break the system. Agents should be able to operate independently and request data as needed.
- **Error Handling**: Implement robust error-handling mechanisms. For example, if the agent cannot retrieve relevant data, it should fall back on alternative sources or provide an alternative response rather than failing silently.

4. Real-Time Adaptation:

- **Monitoring and Feedback Loops**: Regularly monitor the performance of the integration between LangGraph and RAG. This ensures that agents are adapting to real-time data as expected. Implement feedback loops where agents can evaluate the quality of the retrieved data and adjust their decision-making processes accordingly.

7.3 Troubleshooting Common Integration Challenges

When integrating **LangGraph** with **RAG**, there are several common challenges you might encounter. Let's explore these challenges and how to address them.

Challenge 1: Data Retrieval Latency

- **Problem**: Data retrieval from external APIs or databases can introduce latency, especially when the system is dealing with high volumes of requests.
- **Solution**: Implement **asynchronous retrieval** where agents can query external sources in the background while continuing with other tasks. Use **caching** to avoid repeated queries for the same data, and consider using **load balancing** for API calls.

Challenge 2: Data Relevance and Quality

- **Problem**: The retrieved data might not always be relevant or of high quality. This can occur when querying external data sources that are unstructured or not curated for the task at hand.
- **Solution**: Use **semantic search** or **vector search** to improve the relevance of the data being retrieved. Apply **data validation** techniques to ensure the quality of the external data before it is passed to the language model for augmentation.

Challenge 3: Handling Incomplete Data

- **Problem**: Sometimes, the data retrieved from external sources may be incomplete or missing key details.
- **Solution**: Build in fallback mechanisms where agents can either ask the user for more information or use alternative data sources. For example, if the system cannot retrieve current weather data, it could respond with the most recent data available, along with a disclaimer about its freshness.

Challenge 4: Model Overload

- **Problem**: If the language model is tasked with handling too much data or complex queries, it may become **overloaded** and fail to provide timely or relevant answers.
- **Solution**: **Limit the scope** of the data passed to the model. Implement **data filtering** techniques to only pass the most relevant information to the model, reducing its workload and improving response quality.

7.4 Interactive Learning: Integrating LangGraph Agents with an External Knowledge Base

In this interactive example, we will integrate LangGraph agents with an external knowledge base. We will create a system where an agent queries a simple **weather API** for real-time weather information and uses that data to generate a response.

Step 1: Set Up the Knowledge Base

We'll use a weather API like **OpenWeatherMap** to fetch real-time weather data. To get started, sign up for an API key at https://openweathermap.org/api.

Step 2: Define the LangGraph Agent

Here's how to define the LangGraph agent that will query the weather API and generate a response:

```
import requests

# Define the agent class
class WeatherAgent:
    def __init__(self, api_key):
        self.api_key = api_key
        self.base_url =
"http://api.openweathermap.org/data/2.5/weather"

    def get_weather_data(self, city):
```

```python
        url =
f"{self.base_url}?q={city}&appid={self.api_key}&units=metric"
        response = requests.get(url)
        return response.json()

    def generate_response(self, city):
        data = self.get_weather_data(city)
        if data.get("cod") == 200:
            temperature = data["main"]["temp"]
            description = data["weather"][0]["description"]
            return f"The current temperature in {city} is
{temperature}°C with {description}."
        else:
            return "Sorry, I couldn't retrieve weather data
at the moment."

# Initialize the agent with your API key
agent = WeatherAgent(api_key="your_api_key_here")

# Get the weather for a specific city
city = "London"
response = agent.generate_response(city)
print(response)
```

Step 3: Explanation

- The **WeatherAgent** class queries the OpenWeatherMap API using the city name.
- It retrieves the current temperature and weather description and generates a natural language response.
- The agent combines real-time weather data with its language model to produce an informative and relevant answer.

Step 4: Running the Code

When you run this code, you will get output like this:

```
The current temperature in London is 15°C with light rain.
```

This demonstrates how LangGraph agents can integrate with external knowledge bases, retrieve real-time data, and augment their responses accordingly.

7.5 Key Insights

- **LangGraph agents** can enhance their capabilities by integrating with **external knowledge bases** using **RAG** for real-time data retrieval.
- **Best practices** for integration include ensuring efficient data retrieval, maintaining data relevance, and using error handling mechanisms to account for missing or incomplete data.
- **Common integration challenges** include data retrieval latency, relevance of external data, and model overload, all of which can be mitigated with optimization techniques like **caching**, **asynchronous retrieval**, and **semantic search**.
- **LangGraph + RAG** integration allows agents to adapt dynamically to changing environments, improving their decision-making abilities and making them more responsive to real-time information.

7.6 Reflection: What are the challenges of integrating RAG with LangGraph in a production environment?

When considering **RAG integration in production environments**, think about the following challenges:

- **Scalability**: How will the system handle **high traffic** and a large volume of **real-time data retrieval** requests?
- **Data Quality**: How will you ensure that the data retrieved from external sources is of **high quality** and **relevant** to the agent's task?
- **Error Handling**: How will you handle errors, such as **API failures**, **missing data**, or **slow retrieval times**?
- **Latency**: How will you optimize for **minimal latency** when integrating real-time data retrieval into LangGraph agents, ensuring fast response times for users?

Reflecting on these questions will help you understand the complexities of integrating **RAG** into LangGraph at scale and prepare for real-world challenges.

This chapter has provided a comprehensive guide to integrating **LangGraph with RAG**, offering insights into how agents can retrieve real-time data, the best practices for integration, and troubleshooting common challenges. The interactive learning example demonstrated how to integrate a LangGraph agent with an external knowledge base and use real-time data for decision-making. With these skills, you are now equipped to build more powerful, real-time adaptive systems.

Chapter 8: Designing Multi-agent Systems with LangGraph and RAG

In this chapter, we will explore how to design and build **multi-agent systems** (MAS) using **LangGraph** and **Retrieval-Augmented Generation (RAG)**. Multi-agent systems are composed of multiple agents working together to accomplish complex tasks. We will cover the process of defining **agent roles** and **tasks** in a multi-agent workflow, how **LangGraph** facilitates **collaborative task execution**, and how **RAG** enhances **knowledge sharing** among agents. We will also walk through a **mini-project** to create a multi-agent system for task coordination, giving you practical experience in building these systems.

8.1 Defining Agent Roles and Tasks in a Multi-agent Workflow

What are Agent Roles and Tasks?

In a **multi-agent system (MAS)**, each agent has a specific **role** and is responsible for completing certain **tasks**. These roles are defined based on the objectives of the system and are often structured to ensure that each agent works collaboratively with others to achieve a common goal.

- **Agent Role**: The **role** refers to the function or responsibility of an agent within the system. This could include roles such as **data retrieval**, **decision-making**, **task coordination**, or **response generation**.
- **Agent Task**: The **task** refers to the specific work or action an agent is responsible for performing within the system. Tasks could range from simple actions like querying a database, to more complex actions like analyzing data, generating reports, or collaborating with other agents.

Defining Roles in LangGraph

LangGraph provides a modular framework that allows you to **define specific agent roles** and associate them with relevant tasks. Each agent can:

1. **Perform a unique task** (e.g., data retrieval, decision-making, or reporting).
2. **Collaborate with other agents** by sharing information and coordinating actions.

For example, in a **traffic management system**, the roles of the agents could be:

- **Agent 1 (Traffic Light Controller)**: Responsible for adjusting traffic light timings at various intersections based on real-time traffic data.
- **Agent 2 (Traffic Monitor)**: Monitors traffic flow in different regions and shares congestion data with other agents.
- **Agent 3 (Traffic Rerouting)**: Responsible for rerouting traffic based on congestion data shared by Agent 2.

Task Coordination in a Multi-agent System

To ensure that agents can work together efficiently, the system must define the sequence in which tasks are executed. This is known as the **workflow**. In LangGraph, workflows define the **interactions** between agents and ensure that tasks are completed in the correct order.

For example, the workflow in the traffic management system might involve:

1. **Agent 1 (Traffic Light Controller)** adjusts its traffic light timings based on the data it receives from Agent 2 (Traffic Monitor).
2. **Agent 3 (Traffic Rerouting)** takes action based on the data provided by Agent 2 and reroutes traffic accordingly.

8.2 Leveraging LangGraph for Collaborative Task Execution

Collaborative Execution of Tasks

LangGraph's agent-based architecture enables **collaborative task execution**, where agents work together to achieve shared goals. This collaborative behavior is facilitated by:

- **Communication**: Agents exchange information about their state, progress, or required actions, allowing them to make informed decisions and coordinate their tasks.
- **Synchronization**: LangGraph supports synchronization mechanisms, so agents can perform tasks in a timely and coordinated manner.
- **Distributed Decision-Making**: Each agent may be responsible for a part of the decision-making process. LangGraph allows agents to independently make decisions while collaborating to ensure that those decisions align with the system's overall objectives.

Example of Collaborative Execution in LangGraph

In an **e-commerce recommendation system**, different agents might be responsible for different parts of the recommendation process:

1. **Agent 1 (User Profiling)**: Gathers and processes user data to create a profile.
2. **Agent 2 (Product Retrieval)**: Retrieves a list of products based on the user profile.
3. **Agent 3 (Recommendation Generation)**: Combines the user profile and product data to generate personalized product recommendations.

In this system, the agents collaborate by sharing relevant information. **Agent 1** sends user profile data to **Agent 2**, which retrieves relevant products and then sends that data to **Agent 3** to generate the final recommendations.

LangGraph's Workflow Management

LangGraph enables easy management of these workflows by defining which agents need to communicate and in what order. This ensures that tasks are not only executed collaboratively but also in a way that is efficient and prevents bottlenecks.

8.3 Using RAG to Augment Knowledge Sharing Among Agents

Knowledge Sharing Among Agents

In a multi-agent system, **knowledge sharing** is essential for ensuring that agents can make informed decisions and collaborate effectively. **RAG** can play a critical role in enhancing **knowledge sharing** between agents by enabling them to retrieve external data and share that data with other agents in real-time.

How RAG Augments Knowledge Sharing:

1. **Retrieving External Knowledge**: RAG enables agents to **retrieve real-time data** from external sources such as APIs, knowledge bases, or databases, which may not be available within the agent's own knowledge.
2. **Augmenting Responses**: Once the data is retrieved, it can be **shared** with other agents, who can then use it to make decisions or generate responses.
3. **Real-time Data Updates**: RAG ensures that agents work with the most up-to-date information, enhancing their decision-making capabilities and improving the overall collaboration between agents.

Example: Using RAG for Knowledge Sharing in a Multi-agent System

Imagine a **disaster response system** where different agents are responsible for different aspects of the response:

1. **Agent 1 (Weather Monitoring)**: Retrieves real-time weather data to assess potential risks.
2. **Agent 2 (Rescue Coordination)**: Uses the weather data shared by Agent 1 to plan and coordinate rescue operations.

3. **Agent 3 (Resource Allocation)**: Uses the weather data and rescue coordination data to allocate resources effectively.

Here, RAG enables **Agent 1** to retrieve real-time weather data, which is shared with the other agents to ensure that decisions are made using the most up-to-date and accurate information.

8.4 Mini-Project: Building a Multi-agent System for Task Coordination

In this mini-project, we will build a simple **multi-agent system** in LangGraph where agents work together to complete a coordinated task. The system will involve agents that perform **task allocation** and **resource management** in a **project management scenario**.

Step 1: Define the Agents

We will create the following agents:

1. **Agent 1 (Task Allocator)**: Assigns tasks to the appropriate agents based on their skills and availability.
2. **Agent 2 (Resource Manager)**: Manages resources required for each task.
3. **Agent 3 (Task Executor)**: Executes the tasks as assigned by Agent 1 and using resources provided by Agent 2.

Step 2: Define the Workflow

- **Agent 1** allocates tasks to **Agent 3**.
- **Agent 2** provides resources to **Agent 3** for task execution.
- **Agent 3** reports back to **Agent 1** when a task is complete.

Step 3: Implement the Code

Here's a Python implementation of the multi-agent system:

```python
class TaskAllocator:
    def allocate_task(self, task, agent):
        print(f"Task '{task}' allocated to {agent}")
```

```
        return task

class ResourceManager:
    def provide_resources(self, task):
        resources = {"Task 1": "Resource A", "Task 2":
"Resource B"}
        resource = resources.get(task, "No resource
available")
        print(f"Providing {resource} for {task}")
        return resource

class TaskExecutor:
    def execute_task(self, task, resource):
        print(f"Executing {task} with {resource}")
        print(f"{task} completed successfully.")

# Initialize agents
allocator = TaskAllocator()
manager = ResourceManager()
executor = TaskExecutor()

# Workflow example
task = allocator.allocate_task("Task 1", "Agent 3")
resource = manager.provide_resources(task)
executor.execute_task(task, resource)
```

Step 4: Running the Mini-Project

When the system runs, the output will look like:

```
Task 'Task 1' allocated to Agent 3
Providing Resource A for Task 1
Executing Task 1 with Resource A
Task 1 completed successfully.
```

Step 5: Explanation

- **Agent 1 (Task Allocator)** assigns **Task 1** to **Agent 3**.
- **Agent 2 (Resource Manager)** provides **Resource A** required to complete the task.
- **Agent 3 (Task Executor)** executes **Task 1** using **Resource A** and completes it.

This demonstrates a basic workflow where agents collaborate to complete a task in a multi-agent system.

8.5 Key Insights

- **LangGraph agents** play key roles in multi-agent systems, with specific tasks assigned to each agent based on the system's requirements.
- **Task coordination** is essential for ensuring that agents work together effectively. LangGraph allows for easy management of workflows that define how tasks are executed in collaboration.
- **RAG** enhances **knowledge sharing** between agents by enabling real-time data retrieval and augmentation. This ensures that agents have access to the most relevant and up-to-date information.
- **Optimizing collaboration** involves defining clear agent roles, using RAG for external data retrieval, and ensuring that agents can efficiently share knowledge.

8.6 Reflection: How can multi-agent systems be scaled in complex environments?

Consider the following questions to reflect on the scalability of multi-agent systems:

- How can **task distribution** and **coordination** be optimized when dealing with a **larger number of agents**?
- What challenges arise when scaling the number of agents in a system, and how can **communication protocols** be designed to minimize latency?
- How can we handle **conflicting objectives** or **resource contention** among agents in a large-scale system?

Reflecting on these questions will help you understand the complexities of scaling multi-agent systems and prepare for designing solutions that can handle larger, more complex environments.

This chapter has explored the core concepts behind **designing multi-agent systems** using **LangGraph** and **RAG**, covering how to define agent roles, collaborate on tasks, and enhance knowledge sharing. The mini-project provided hands-on experience in creating a simple multi-agent system. With these insights, you are now equipped to design and build scalable, efficient, and collaborative multi-agent systems using LangGraph and RAG.

Chapter 9: Implementing Multi-Agent Collaboration

In this chapter, we will explore the critical aspects of **multi-agent collaboration**, focusing on techniques for **communication**, **coordination**, and **task distribution** among agents. We will also dive into more complex topics like **conflict resolution**, **consensus building**, and ensuring **efficiency and scalability** within multi-agent systems. The chapter includes a hands-on challenge where we will build a **real-time decision-making system** with multiple agents working together. By the end of this chapter, you will have a comprehensive understanding of how to implement successful collaboration strategies in multi-agent systems.

9.1 Techniques for Agent Communication and Coordination

Effective Communication in Multi-agent Systems

In multi-agent systems, communication is the key to ensuring that agents work together efficiently. Since each agent in a MAS often has partial knowledge of the system, communication allows them to share information and coordinate their actions. There are two primary types of communication used in multi-agent systems:

1. **Synchronous Communication**:
   - In synchronous communication, agents **exchange messages** and wait for responses before proceeding.
   - Example: A task allocation system where Agent A sends a request to Agent B for assistance. Agent B waits to process the request before proceeding.

   Advantages: Ensures that agents receive confirmation or data before proceeding to the next task, reducing the chance of errors.

   Disadvantages: It can slow down the system if the agents are waiting for long periods for a response, leading to potential inefficiencies.

2. **Asynchronous Communication**:
    o In asynchronous communication, agents send messages and **continue working** without waiting for a response. Responses are handled as soon as they arrive.
    o Example: In a logistics system, an agent may send a message requesting updated data on vehicle availability but continue with other tasks without waiting for a response.

Advantages: More efficient as agents do not need to wait for each other's responses, allowing for faster processing.

Disadvantages: There is a potential for **mismatched data** or conflicts, as responses may arrive out of order or too late to be useful.

Communication Protocols

To ensure effective communication, agents must adhere to a **communication protocol**. The protocol defines the structure of the messages and the rules for interaction, ensuring agents understand each other's intents and states. Common protocols include:

- **FIPA-ACL (Foundation for Intelligent Physical Agents – Agent Communication Language)**: A standard for agent communication that allows agents to send messages with specific **performative** types (e.g., query, request, inform).
- **KQML (Knowledge Query and Manipulation Language)**: Another language for agent communication, designed for knowledge sharing between agents.
- **Custom Protocols**: Some multi-agent systems use **custom protocols** depending on the complexity of the task or the environment.

9.2 Conflict Resolution and Consensus Building Among Agents

Understanding Conflicts in Multi-agent Systems

In multi-agent systems, conflicts may arise due to **competing goals**, **resource limitations**, or differences in **knowledge**. Managing these conflicts effectively is essential for ensuring smooth collaboration among agents.

Types of Conflicts:

1. **Goal Conflicts**: Occur when agents pursue objectives that are incompatible with one another. For example, two agents may be competing for the same resource or trying to optimize a different aspect of a shared goal.
2. **Resource Conflicts**: Arise when agents compete for limited resources, such as bandwidth, processing power, or access to data.
3. **Information Conflicts**: Happen when agents receive conflicting information or have **incomplete knowledge** about the system or environment.

Consensus Building

Consensus building is the process of ensuring that agents in a system agree on a common course of action or decision, especially when there are conflicts. The goal is to find a mutually acceptable solution that satisfies all (or most) agents' objectives.

Techniques for Consensus Building:

1. **Voting Mechanisms**: Agents vote on decisions, and the option with the most votes is chosen. This is a **democratic** approach that ensures all agents have a say in the decision-making process.
   - Example: In a **resource allocation system**, agents might vote on which task should be prioritized based on available resources.
2. **Negotiation**: Agents negotiate with each other to come to a mutually beneficial solution. This could involve **bargaining** or offering **compromise solutions**.

o   Example: Two agents might negotiate to share resources (e.g., time slots or processing power) to complete their tasks.

3. **Mediation**: A third-party agent acts as a mediator, helping other agents resolve conflicts by suggesting **fair solutions**.
   o   Example: A **mediator agent** could help resolve a conflict between two agents over which task should be prioritized based on resource availability.

Example:

Consider a multi-agent **robotic team** working on an assembly line:

- **Agent 1** (a robotic arm) might want to move to an area to perform a task, while **Agent 2** (another robotic arm) is already there.
- To resolve this, the two agents might negotiate to determine which task should be completed first, or they might use a **voting system** to prioritize the most critical task.

9.3 Task Distribution: Ensuring Efficiency and Scalability

The Importance of Task Distribution

In large-scale multi-agent systems, **task distribution** ensures that tasks are evenly spread among agents, leading to improved **efficiency** and **scalability**. Proper task distribution helps avoid bottlenecks, reduces idle time for agents, and allows the system to handle **more complex tasks** as the number of agents increases.

Techniques for Efficient Task Distribution:

1. **Round-Robin Scheduling**:
   o   Tasks are distributed evenly among agents in a **cyclic manner**, ensuring each agent gets an equal share of the workload.
   o   Example: In a **cloud computing system**, each agent (or worker) could be assigned a job in turn, preventing any single worker from becoming overloaded.

2. **Task Prioritization**:
   - Tasks are distributed based on their **priority**, ensuring that important tasks are handled first. This could be based on predefined rules or real-time data.
   - Example: In a **logistics system**, priority tasks (such as urgent deliveries) are assigned to the most capable agents.
3. **Dynamic Task Assignment**:
   - Task assignment is based on the **current state** of the system, such as agent availability, workload, and the environment. This ensures that agents are assigned tasks that match their capabilities at any given time.
   - Example: In a **distributed sensor network**, agents with fewer tasks or available processing power may take on additional work.
4. **Load Balancing**:
   - Distribute tasks in a way that minimizes the overall **workload variance** among agents, ensuring that no agent becomes overloaded.
   - Example: A **load-balancing algorithm** could be used to assign tasks to agents in a cloud-based system to prevent certain servers from becoming bottlenecks.

Scalability:

Task distribution is key to ensuring that multi-agent systems scale efficiently as the number of agents increases. Proper distribution can prevent **overhead** and ensure the system can handle additional agents or tasks without performance degradation.

9.4 Challenge: Building a Multi-agent System for Real-Time Decision Making

In this challenge, we will implement a simple multi-agent system where agents work together to make real-time decisions. We will simulate a **traffic management system**, where agents must coordinate their actions based on real-time traffic data.

Step 1: Define the Agents

We will define the following agents:

1. **Agent 1 (Traffic Data Collector)**: Collects real-time traffic data from external sources (e.g., sensors, cameras).
2. **Agent 2 (Traffic Light Controller)**: Uses the data from Agent 1 to adjust traffic light timings.
3. **Agent 3 (Traffic Flow Optimizer)**: Analyzes the traffic data to determine the optimal routes for vehicles.

Step 2: Define the Workflow

- **Agent 1** collects real-time traffic data.
- **Agent 2** adjusts the traffic lights based on the collected data.
- **Agent 3** analyzes the data and recommends routes for vehicles to minimize congestion.

Step 3: Implement the Code

```python
import random
import time

# Define agents
class TrafficDataCollector:
    def collect_data(self):
        data = random.randint(10, 100)  # Simulate traffic
data (vehicle count)
        print(f"TrafficDataCollector: Collected traffic data:
{data} vehicles")
        return data

class TrafficLightController:
    def adjust_traffic_lights(self, data):
        if data > 80:
            print("TrafficLightController: Adjusting traffic
lights to green for longer duration.")
        else:
            print("TrafficLightController: Adjusting traffic
lights to normal.")

class TrafficFlowOptimizer:
    def recommend_routes(self, data):
        if data > 80:
            print("TrafficFlowOptimizer: Recommending
alternate routes to avoid congestion.")
        else:
            print("TrafficFlowOptimizer: Traffic flow is
normal, no rerouting needed.")
```

```python
# Create agents
collector = TrafficDataCollector()
controller = TrafficLightController()
optimizer = TrafficFlowOptimizer()

# Simulate real-time decision making
for _ in range(5):
    traffic_data = collector.collect_data()
    controller.adjust_traffic_lights(traffic_data)
    optimizer.recommend_routes(traffic_data)
    time.sleep(2)  # Simulate real-time data collection
```

Step 4: Explanation

- **Agent 1** (TrafficDataCollector) collects random traffic data (simulating real-time vehicle count).
- **Agent 2** (TrafficLightController) adjusts the traffic light timings based on the data.
- **Agent 3** (TrafficFlowOptimizer) recommends alternate routes when traffic is heavy.

Step 5: Running the Challenge

When the system runs, it will output something like:

```
TrafficDataCollector: Collected traffic data: 92 vehicles
TrafficLightController: Adjusting traffic lights to green for
longer duration.
TrafficFlowOptimizer: Recommending alternate routes to avoid
congestion.
```

9.5 Key Insights

- **Agent communication and coordination** are crucial for ensuring that agents work together efficiently, especially in real-time decision-making systems.
- **Conflict resolution** and **consensus building** help ensure that agents can collaborate even when their goals or actions conflict.
- **Task distribution** is essential for ensuring that the system remains efficient and scalable, especially as the number of agents increases.
- Relying on **real-time data** and **dynamic task allocation** enables agents to adapt quickly to changes in the environment.

9.6 Reflection: What methods would you use to ensure agents work together harmoniously in large systems?

When considering **large-scale multi-agent systems**, think about the following methods:

- **Decentralized Control**: Allow agents to make decisions autonomously while maintaining coordination through shared protocols and workflows.
- **Effective Communication**: Ensure that communication is clear, efficient, and timely between agents. Consider using **event-driven communication** to notify agents of important changes.
- **Consensus Mechanisms**: Implement systems for **conflict resolution** and **decision-making**, such as voting, negotiation, or arbitration, to ensure agents can resolve disagreements.
- **Task Distribution Algorithms**: Use load balancing and dynamic task allocation strategies to ensure tasks are distributed effectively among agents, even as the system scales.

Reflecting on these methods will help you design and manage large-scale multi-agent systems that work harmoniously and efficiently.

This chapter has provided an in-depth guide to **implementing multi-agent collaboration**, focusing on communication, coordination, task distribution, and conflict resolution. We covered a **real-time decision-making system** example and explored techniques for ensuring agents can work together harmoniously in complex environments. With these insights, you are now well-equipped to design, implement, and scale multi-agent systems for various applications.

Chapter 10: Optimizing Multi-agent Systems for Scalability

In this chapter, we will focus on the critical aspects of **scaling** and **optimizing multi-agent systems (MAS)** that leverage **LangGraph** and **Retrieval-Augmented Generation (RAG)**. These systems must be efficient and responsive, especially when dealing with **large-scale applications**. We will discuss how to scale LangGraph RAG systems, the key performance metrics to monitor, and techniques for optimizing data retrieval to reduce latency and improve response times. A mini-project will provide hands-on experience in optimizing a multi-agent system for high-performance scenarios. By the end of this chapter, you will have a deeper understanding of how to measure and optimize the scalability of MAS.

10.1 Scaling LangGraph RAG Systems for Large-Scale Applications

Challenges in Scaling Multi-agent Systems

As multi-agent systems grow, there are several challenges to consider:

- **Communication Overhead**: As the number of agents increases, the communication cost between them also increases. Handling large volumes of messages and interactions can slow down the system.
- **Data Retrieval Bottlenecks**: In systems that integrate RAG, the external data retrieval process can become a bottleneck if not optimized.
- **Load Balancing**: Distributing tasks efficiently across a large number of agents to prevent some agents from becoming overloaded while others are idle.
- **Concurrency**: Ensuring that agents can operate simultaneously without interfering with each other.

Scaling Strategies for LangGraph RAG Systems

To scale LangGraph RAG systems effectively, you need to focus on both the **architecture** and the **data flow**.

1. Distributed Agent Management

One effective approach to scaling LangGraph RAG systems is to implement **distributed agent management**. This involves running agents across multiple machines or servers to distribute the load. Key aspects of distributed agent management include:

- **Load Balancing**: Ensure that the workload is evenly distributed across all agents. This reduces the risk of system slowdowns or failures due to overburdened agents.
- **Distributed Data Storage**: Use distributed databases or cloud-based storage solutions (like **Amazon S3**, **Google Cloud Storage**, or **Azure Blob Storage**) to store knowledge graphs or other shared data. This allows all agents to access the data from different locations without significant latency.

2. Horizontal Scaling

To support a growing number of agents, the system can be horizontally scaled. This means adding more instances of agents to handle more tasks. Key steps to achieving horizontal scaling include:

- **Containerization**: Using **Docker** containers to deploy agents across multiple nodes or machines ensures that each agent instance is isolated and can be scaled independently.
- **Kubernetes**: For managing large numbers of containers, **Kubernetes** provides an orchestration platform that can automate the deployment, scaling, and management of containers.

3. Caching and Pre-fetching

To avoid frequent data retrieval delays, it is important to implement **caching** and **pre-fetching**:

- **Cache Frequently Used Data**: Cache common queries and results from external sources so that agents don't have to fetch the same data repeatedly.

- **Data Pre-fetching**: Pre-fetch certain data before it's needed based on the system's anticipated needs (e.g., based on previous user queries or agent activities).

4. Distributed RAG Retrieval

For RAG-based systems, scaling the retrieval process is crucial:

- **Distributed Indexing**: Use distributed search engines like **Elasticsearch** or **Apache Solr** to index and search external data. These engines allow for fast retrieval across large datasets.
- **Vector Search**: Use vector-based search techniques (e.g., **FAISS** or **Annoy**) to enable fast and scalable retrieval of semantically relevant data, especially when querying large knowledge graphs.

10.2 Performance Metrics: Measuring Efficiency and Latency

Key Performance Metrics

When optimizing multi-agent systems, it's essential to track several key performance metrics to ensure that the system is running efficiently and meeting real-time performance goals. These metrics include:

1. Latency

- **Definition**: Latency is the time it takes for the system to process a request and deliver a response.
- **Importance**: Low latency is crucial for real-time decision-making systems, such as traffic management or financial trading.
- **Optimization**: To reduce latency, optimize both the communication between agents and the retrieval process. This can be done by using efficient protocols and minimizing data transfer times.

2. Throughput

- **Definition**: Throughput measures the number of requests or tasks the system can handle within a specific time frame.

- **Importance**: High throughput is important for handling large numbers of simultaneous requests, especially in large-scale applications.
- **Optimization**: Distribute tasks across agents and use load balancing to maximize throughput. Parallel processing can also improve throughput.

3. Resource Utilization

- **Definition**: Resource utilization tracks how efficiently the system uses computing resources such as CPU, memory, and network bandwidth.
- **Importance**: Efficient resource usage helps ensure that the system can handle increased demand without becoming inefficient or costly.
- **Optimization**: Use efficient algorithms and data structures, and scale the system horizontally to prevent any one machine from becoming a bottleneck.

4. Scalability

- **Definition**: Scalability is the system's ability to grow and handle increased load by adding resources (such as additional agents or servers).
- **Importance**: A scalable system can handle increasing amounts of data or users without degrading performance.
- **Optimization**: Design the system to be easily **horizontal scalable**, using distributed technologies like Kubernetes and load balancing.

5. Response Time

- **Definition**: Response time measures how long it takes for the system to respond to a query or action.
- **Importance**: Low response time is crucial for ensuring that users and agents can interact with the system in real-time.
- **Optimization**: Minimize network latency, optimize agent communication protocols, and implement caching for faster responses.

10.3 Optimizing Data Retrieval for Faster Response Times

Techniques for Data Retrieval Optimization

The data retrieval process in **RAG systems** can become a bottleneck if not optimized properly. Here are a few techniques to ensure faster retrieval:

1. Caching Results

Cache the results of frequently queried data to avoid repetitive searches and reduce retrieval time. By caching the output of common queries (such as the latest stock prices or frequently accessed knowledge graph nodes), agents can quickly access this data without having to query external sources repeatedly.

```
cache = {}

def get_cached_data(query):
    if query in cache:
        return cache[query]
    else:
        # Simulate data retrieval from an API
        data = fetch_data_from_api(query)
        cache[query] = data
        return data

def fetch_data_from_api(query):
    # Simulate fetching data from an external source
    return f"Data for {query}"
```

2. Using In-memory Databases

In-memory databases like **Redis** can be used to cache data at a much faster speed than traditional disk-based databases. Redis can store frequently accessed data in **memory**, providing extremely fast access times.

```
import redis

# Initialize Redis client
redis_client = redis.StrictRedis(host='localhost', port=6379,
db=0)

def get_cached_data_from_redis(query):
    cached_data = redis_client.get(query)
```

```
if cached_data:
    return cached_data.decode('utf-8')
else:
    # Fetch from external source if not in cache
    data = fetch_data_from_api(query)
    redis_client.set(query, data)
    return data
```

3. Asynchronous Data Fetching

For external data sources with high latency, consider using **asynchronous techniques** to fetch data in parallel while other agents continue working.

```
import asyncio

async def fetch_data(query):
    # Simulate asynchronous data fetching from an API
    await asyncio.sleep(1)  # Simulate delay
    return f"Fetched {query}"

async def main():
    queries = ["query1", "query2", "query3"]
    tasks = [fetch_data(query) for query in queries]
    results = await asyncio.gather(*tasks)
    print(results)

asyncio.run(main())
```

4. Distributed Retrieval Systems

When dealing with massive datasets, a distributed retrieval system like **Elasticsearch** or **Apache Solr** can provide high-performance querying and retrieval capabilities. These systems are optimized for searching large volumes of data across distributed nodes, offering quick and accurate retrieval even at scale.

10.4 Mini-Project: Optimizing a Multi-agent System for High-Performance Scenarios

In this mini-project, we will build a simple **multi-agent system** and implement optimizations for performance, focusing on **data retrieval** and **scalability**.

Step 1: Define the Agents

We will define a **data retrieval agent** that fetches information from an external API, caches the results, and uses that data to make decisions. Additionally, we will simulate a **load balancing agent** to distribute tasks evenly.

Step 2: Implement Caching and Load Balancing

We'll use **Redis** for caching and **asyncio** for fetching data asynchronously.

```python
import asyncio
import redis

# Initialize Redis client
redis_client = redis.StrictRedis(host='localhost', port=6379,
db=0)

# Simulate external API fetching
async def fetch_data(query):
    await asyncio.sleep(1)   # Simulate delay
    return f"Fetched {query}"

def get_cached_data(query):
    cached_data = redis_client.get(query)
    if cached_data:
        return cached_data.decode('utf-8')
    else:
        # Fetch from external source
        data = asyncio.run(fetch_data(query))
        redis_client.set(query, data)
        return data

# Load balancing example: Distribute queries evenly
agents = ["Agent 1", "Agent 2", "Agent 3"]
queries = ["query1", "query2", "query3"]

# Distribute queries to agents
for i, query in enumerate(queries):
    agent = agents[i % len(agents)]
    print(f"{agent} handling {query}:
{get_cached_data(query)}")
```

Step 3: Running the Mini-Project

Running this project will output:

```
Agent 1 handling query1: Fetched query1
Agent 2 handling query2: Fetched query2
Agent 3 handling query3: Fetched query3
```

Step 4: Explanation

- **Caching** ensures that data retrieval is fast for repeated queries.
- **Load balancing** evenly distributes tasks across available agents to avoid overloading any single agent.

10.5 Key Insights

- **Scalability** is crucial when building large-scale systems. Techniques like distributed agent management, caching, and horizontal scaling help improve performance.
- **Performance metrics** such as latency, throughput, and resource utilization must be tracked to ensure that multi-agent systems remain efficient.
- **Optimizing data retrieval** through caching, asynchronous fetching, and using distributed systems like Elasticsearch can significantly improve response times and scalability.

10.6 Reflection: How would you measure the performance and efficiency of a multi-agent system?

To measure the **performance** and **efficiency** of a multi-agent system, consider the following:

- **Latency**: How long does it take for the system to respond to requests? Consider whether **real-time responses** are critical.
- **Throughput**: How many requests or tasks can the system handle per unit of time? Consider whether high throughput is needed in your system.
- **Resource Utilization**: How efficiently does the system use computing resources like CPU, memory, and network bandwidth?

- **Scalability**: How well does the system scale when more agents or tasks are added? Test the system's ability to handle increasing demand without performance degradation.

These insights will help you design and optimize multi-agent systems for real-world, large-scale applications.

This chapter has provided an in-depth look at **optimizing multi-agent systems** for scalability, including techniques for data retrieval, performance metrics, and best practices for improving system efficiency. The mini-project helped demonstrate how to implement these concepts in a practical context. By applying these strategies, you will be able to design multi-agent systems that can scale efficiently while maintaining high performance.

Chapter 11: Advanced Multi-agent System Architectures

In this chapter, we will delve into advanced **multi-agent system (MAS) architectures**, focusing on building **hierarchical and autonomous** systems, designing **distributed LangGraph architectures**, and integrating MAS with **IoT** (Internet of Things) and **Edge Computing** for **real-time decision-making**. We will also work through a challenging exercise where we design a **decentralized multi-agent system** for a **smart city**. By the end of this chapter, you will have a deep understanding of advanced architectures in multi-agent systems and how to apply these concepts in real-world scenarios.

11.1 Building Hierarchical and Autonomous Agent Systems

What are Hierarchical and Autonomous Agent Systems?

In a **multi-agent system**, agents can be structured in different ways, depending on the complexity and requirements of the application. Two common architectures are **hierarchical systems** and **autonomous agent systems**.

1. Hierarchical Agent Systems

In **hierarchical agent systems**, agents are organized into layers, where higher-level agents supervise or control lower-level agents. This architecture is useful in systems that require **centralized decision-making** or need to manage a large number of agents efficiently.

- **Upper-Level Agents**: These agents manage higher-level goals and decisions and may supervise lower-level agents or coordinate different tasks.
- **Lower-Level Agents**: These agents handle specific tasks, often with less autonomy. They are managed by upper-level agents but may also communicate with other agents to complete their work.

Example: Consider a **logistics system** where high-level agents manage global distribution strategies, while lower-level agents are responsible for warehouse management and transportation optimization.

2. Autonomous Agent Systems

In **autonomous agent systems**, each agent acts independently, with its own decision-making capabilities. Agents in such systems do not rely on a central authority, making them more flexible and capable of reacting to environmental changes in real-time.

- **Decentralized Decision-Making**: Each agent in an autonomous system can make decisions based on its local knowledge and environmental factors. This reduces bottlenecks and enables the system to scale efficiently.
- **Self-Organizing**: These systems often exhibit **emergent behaviors**, where agents' interactions give rise to complex behaviors without centralized control.

Example: In an **autonomous vehicle system**, each vehicle (agent) independently decides its path, speed, and interactions with other vehicles without a central control system.

Combining Hierarchical and Autonomous Architectures

It's possible to combine hierarchical and autonomous architectures to take advantage of the strengths of both. For example:

- A **hierarchical structure** can be used for global coordination, while **autonomous agents** handle local tasks.
- **Task Decomposition**: Higher-level agents can break down complex tasks into smaller, manageable tasks, which are then handled by autonomous agents at the lower levels.

11.2 Designing Distributed LangGraph Architectures

What is Distributed LangGraph Architecture?

A **distributed LangGraph architecture** involves distributing LangGraph agents across multiple machines or nodes to handle larger, more complex systems. Distributed systems are essential for building scalable applications, as they allow you to **divide and conquer** tasks, making it easier to handle increased workloads.

Key Components of Distributed LangGraph Architectures:

1. **Distributed Agents**: Each agent in the system can be deployed across different machines or containers. This enables parallel execution and resource sharing.
   - Example: In a **cloud-based application**, agents can run on separate instances, each performing different tasks while communicating with each other.
2. **Distributed Knowledge Graphs**: In large systems, the knowledge graph might also need to be distributed to ensure that data is accessible across different nodes. Distributed databases, such as **Neo4j** (with clustering support), or cloud-based storage like **Amazon S3** or **Google Cloud Storage**, can be used to store and share the knowledge graph data.
3. **Communication Infrastructure**: For distributed LangGraph systems, efficient **communication protocols** (like **MQTT**, **gRPC**, or **HTTP/REST APIs**) must be in place to ensure smooth interaction between agents located on different machines.
4. **Data Consistency and Synchronization**: In distributed systems, it is essential to maintain **data consistency** across different agents. Techniques like **event sourcing** or **distributed transactions** can be used to ensure that all agents are working with up-to-date and consistent data.

Advantages of Distributed LangGraph Architectures:

- **Scalability**: By distributing the workload, you can easily scale the system to handle more agents and tasks.

- **Fault Tolerance**: Distributing agents across multiple nodes ensures that if one agent or node fails, the system can still function.
- **Improved Performance**: Distributed systems allow for better load balancing, reducing the chances of any one agent or machine becoming a bottleneck.

11.3 Integration with IoT and Edge Computing for Real-Time Decision Making

Integrating MAS with IoT

Internet of Things (IoT) refers to the network of physical devices, vehicles, appliances, and other objects embedded with sensors, software, and network connectivity that enable them to collect and exchange data. Integrating **IoT** with multi-agent systems enhances the system's ability to make **real-time decisions** based on data from the physical world.

- **Real-time Data Acquisition**: IoT devices collect data (e.g., sensor readings, location data) and send it to agents, which can then make decisions or perform tasks based on that data.
- **Autonomous Decision-Making**: Agents can analyze the data provided by IoT devices in real-time and take autonomous actions, such as adjusting traffic lights in a smart city or optimizing energy consumption in a smart grid.

Example: A smart city system where IoT devices (e.g., traffic sensors, smart meters, weather stations) provide data to multi-agent systems that control traffic, manage energy, and optimize urban infrastructure.

Edge Computing for Real-Time Decision Making

Edge computing involves processing data closer to the source (e.g., at the "edge" of the network) rather than sending it all to a centralized server. This is particularly important in systems that require **low-latency decision-making** or where bandwidth is limited.

- **Low Latency**: Edge computing ensures that data processing happens near the IoT devices, which drastically reduces response times and makes the system more responsive.
- **Data Filtering and Pre-processing**: With edge computing, data can be filtered or pre-processed before it is sent to the cloud or central system, reducing the amount of data transmitted and ensuring faster decisions.

Example: In a smart factory, IoT sensors detect machinery malfunctions and send data to edge devices, which analyze the data and trigger repairs or adjustments locally, ensuring minimal downtime.

11.4 Advanced Challenge: Designing a Decentralized Multi-agent System for a Smart City

Challenge Objective:

Design a **decentralized multi-agent system** that coordinates **smart city** infrastructure. The system will include agents responsible for **traffic management**, **energy optimization**, and **waste management**. Each agent will make real-time decisions based on data from **IoT devices** (e.g., traffic sensors, energy meters, waste bins).

Step 1: Define the Agents

1. **Agent 1 (Traffic Management Agent)**: Manages traffic lights and flow based on real-time data from traffic sensors.
2. **Agent 2 (Energy Optimization Agent)**: Optimizes energy usage in the city by controlling smart meters and energy storage systems.
3. **Agent 3 (Waste Management Agent)**: Monitors waste levels in smart bins and coordinates waste collection schedules.

Step 2: Define the Workflow

1. **Agent 1** (Traffic Management) adjusts traffic flow based on real-time data from IoT sensors.

2. **Agent 2** (Energy Optimization) adjusts energy usage based on data from smart meters, ensuring that power demand and supply are balanced.
3. **Agent 3** (Waste Management) collects data from IoT waste bins and schedules garbage collection based on fill levels.

Step 3: Implement the Code

```python
import random
import time

# Define agents
class TrafficAgent:
    def manage_traffic(self):
        traffic_data = random.randint(50, 200)  # Simulate
traffic data (vehicle count)
        print(f"TrafficAgent: Adjusting traffic lights based
on {traffic_data} vehicles.")

class EnergyAgent:
    def optimize_energy(self):
        energy_data = random.randint(10, 100)  # Simulate
energy data (power usage)
        print(f"EnergyAgent: Optimizing energy consumption
with {energy_data}% usage.")

class WasteAgent:
    def manage_waste(self):
        waste_data = random.randint(10, 50)  # Simulate waste
data (bin fill percentage)
        print(f"WasteAgent: Scheduling garbage collection
with {waste_data}% fill.")

# Create agents
traffic_agent = TrafficAgent()
energy_agent = EnergyAgent()
waste_agent = WasteAgent()

# Simulate real-time decision-making
for _ in range(5):
    traffic_agent.manage_traffic()
    energy_agent.optimize_energy()
    waste_agent.manage_waste()
    time.sleep(2)  # Simulate real-time data collection
```

Step 4: Running the Challenge

Running this code will simulate agents interacting in real-time:

```
TrafficAgent: Adjusting traffic lights based on 127 vehicles.
EnergyAgent: Optimizing energy consumption with 80% usage.
WasteAgent: Scheduling garbage collection with 35% fill.
```

Step 5: Explanation

- Each agent makes real-time decisions based on data collected from IoT devices.
- The agents work autonomously but share critical information, such as traffic or waste data, to ensure smooth system operation.

11.5 Key Insights

- **Hierarchical and autonomous systems** each have their strengths. Hierarchical systems are good for centralized control, while autonomous systems offer flexibility and adaptability.
- **Distributed LangGraph architectures** allow for scaling, fault tolerance, and efficient data access across multiple agents and nodes.
- Integrating **IoT** and **edge computing** into multi-agent systems improves **real-time decision-making** by reducing latency and enhancing data accuracy.
- Building **decentralized multi-agent systems** for large-scale applications like smart cities allows for **autonomous operation**, scalability, and responsiveness to real-time events.

11.6 Reflection: What are the benefits of distributed systems over centralized systems in multi-agent networks?

Reflecting on the benefits of distributed systems in multi-agent networks:

- **Scalability**: Distributed systems can scale by simply adding more nodes or agents. In contrast, centralized systems may become bottlenecked as they grow.
- **Fault Tolerance**: Distributed systems are more robust because failure in one agent or node does not bring down the entire system. Centralized systems are more prone to single points of failure.
- **Decentralized Decision-Making**: Agents in distributed systems can make decisions locally, reducing the need for constant communication with a central authority and allowing for quicker responses.
- **Efficiency**: Distributed systems can balance workloads across multiple agents, ensuring that no single agent or node becomes overloaded.

Reflecting on these factors can help you understand when to choose **distributed architectures** over **centralized systems** in your multi-agent network designs.

This chapter has introduced advanced **multi-agent system architectures**, including hierarchical and autonomous systems, distributed LangGraph architectures, and integration with IoT and edge computing. Through a real-world **smart city challenge**, we explored how to design and implement decentralized systems. These insights will help you design and optimize robust, scalable, and efficient multi-agent systems.

Chapter 12: Case Study 1: Building a Customer Support Agent System

In this chapter, we will design a **multi-agent system** for **automated customer support** using **LangGraph** and **Retrieval-Augmented Generation (RAG)**. We will cover how to build a system that efficiently answers customer queries, integrates real-time knowledge retrieval, and tracks customer interactions using **knowledge graphs**. Additionally, we will walk through an **end-to-end tutorial** where we will implement the system step-by-step. By the end of the chapter, you will have the tools and understanding to build a robust customer support agent system with LangGraph and RAG.

12.1 Designing a Multi-agent System for Automated Customer Support

Overview of Automated Customer Support Systems

Automated customer support systems are designed to handle customer inquiries and issues without the need for human intervention. A multi-agent system (MAS) allows different agents to specialize in various tasks within the customer support process, resulting in a more efficient and scalable solution.

Key Components of the System:

1. **Customer Query Agent**:
   o This agent receives customer queries and determines the best way to process them, such as directing the query to a specific support agent or answering the query directly.
2. **Information Retrieval Agent**:
   o This agent retrieves information from knowledge sources (e.g., internal databases, FAQs, or knowledge graphs) to help answer customer questions.
3. **Response Generation Agent**:

      o   This agent generates the final response to the customer based on the retrieved information and the context of the query.
4. **Feedback Collection Agent**:
      o   After providing a solution, this agent collects feedback from the customer to improve the system's performance and understanding.

Process Flow:

1. **Query Reception**: The customer submits a query via a chat interface or voice assistant.
2. **Query Processing**: The **Customer Query Agent** processes the query, identifying its type (e.g., technical issue, product inquiry, etc.).
3. **Knowledge Retrieval**: The **Information Retrieval Agent** accesses the knowledge base (e.g., FAQ, previous interactions) to find relevant information.
4. **Response Generation**: The **Response Generation Agent** synthesizes the retrieved data and constructs a reply for the customer.
5. **Customer Feedback**: After the response is sent, the **Feedback Collection Agent** asks the customer for feedback to evaluate the system's accuracy and performance.

This multi-agent structure allows for specialized agents to collaborate on solving customer queries quickly and effectively.

12.2 Integrating RAG for Dynamic Knowledge Retrieval in Real-Time Support

What is Retrieval-Augmented Generation (RAG)?

Retrieval-Augmented Generation (RAG) is a powerful approach where the generation model (e.g., GPT, BERT) is augmented with external knowledge by retrieving relevant information from databases or knowledge sources. This is particularly useful in scenarios where the system needs to handle a vast amount of data and provide dynamic, real-time responses to customer queries.

Why Use RAG for Customer Support?

- **Dynamic Knowledge Retrieval**: By integrating RAG, the system can **retrieve real-time information** from an up-to-date knowledge base, ensuring that customers receive accurate and current responses.
- **Scalability**: As customer queries become more complex, RAG helps generate better responses by pulling in additional context from external sources.
- **Improved Accuracy**: RAG improves the response quality by incorporating detailed and specific information into the generation process.

How RAG Works in the Customer Support System:

1. **Customer Query**: A customer asks a question, such as "What is the status of my order?"
2. **Data Retrieval**: The **Information Retrieval Agent** fetches relevant information from an order management system, such as the current status of the order, shipping details, etc.
3. **Augmented Response**: The **Response Generation Agent** augments the query with the retrieved information, providing a detailed and personalized response, such as, "Your order is currently being processed and will ship in 2-3 business days."
4. **Final Response**: The response is sent back to the customer.

By using RAG, the system can quickly and accurately retrieve relevant data, even when the knowledge base contains a large amount of complex, real-time data.

12.3 Tracking Customer Interactions via Knowledge Graphs

What is a Knowledge Graph?

A **knowledge graph** is a powerful data structure used to represent relationships between entities (such as customers, products, and services) and their attributes. In the context of customer support, a knowledge graph can store:

- Customer profiles (e.g., name, contact details, order history).
- Product details (e.g., specifications, warranty information).

- Interaction history (e.g., past support queries, resolutions).

Why Track Customer Interactions Using Knowledge Graphs?

- **Personalization**: Knowledge graphs help store customer interaction history and preferences, enabling the system to provide personalized responses.
- **Contextual Understanding**: By analyzing the relationships between different entities, the system can better understand the context of a customer's query.
- **Analytics**: A knowledge graph can help identify trends in customer behavior and frequently asked questions, improving the support system's overall efficiency.

Example of Customer Interaction Tracking:

Consider a scenario where a customer asks about a product's warranty status. The knowledge graph can store the relationship between the customer and the product, allowing the system to quickly retrieve and respond with the relevant warranty information.

12.4 End-to-End Tutorial: Building a Customer Support System with LangGraph and RAG

Step 1: Setting Up the Environment

Before we start building, ensure you have the following dependencies installed:

- Python 3.7+
- LangGraph library
- RAG-enabled model (e.g., Hugging Face's transformers library)
- Redis (for caching)
- Requests (for API calls)

Install the necessary packages using pip:

```
pip install langgraph transformers redis requests
```

Step 2: Define the Agents

We will define three main agents: the **Customer Query Agent**, the **Information Retrieval Agent**, and the **Response Generation Agent**.

Customer Query Agent:

This agent processes the customer's input, determines its intent, and directs the query to the appropriate agents.

```
class CustomerQueryAgent:
    def process_query(self, query):
        print(f"Processing query: {query}")
        # For simplicity, we assume it's always a product-
related query
        return "product_related_query"
```

Information Retrieval Agent:

This agent retrieves relevant product details from a simulated external database (could be an API, knowledge base, or knowledge graph).

```
import requests

class InfoRetrievalAgent:
    def retrieve_data(self, query):
        # Simulating an external API call to get product data
        product_data = {"product_name": "Smartphone",
"warranty": "2 years", "stock_status": "In stock"}
        print(f"Retrieving data for query: {query}")
        return product_data
```

Response Generation Agent:

This agent uses **RAG** to generate a response based on the retrieved data.

```
from transformers import pipeline

class ResponseGenerationAgent:
    def __init__(self):
        self.generator = pipeline("text-generation",
model="gpt2")

    def generate_response(self, query, retrieved_data):
```

```
        context = f"{query} -
{retrieved_data['product_name']} is available with
{retrieved_data['warranty']} warranty."
        response = self.generator(context, max_length=50)
        print(f"Generated response:
{response[0]['generated_text']}")
        return response[0]['generated_text']
```

Step 3: Connect the Agents

Now, we will connect the agents to handle a customer's query and generate a response.

```
# Instantiate the agents
customer_agent = CustomerQueryAgent()
retrieval_agent = InfoRetrievalAgent()
response_agent = ResponseGenerationAgent()

# Simulate a customer query
customer_query = "Can you tell me about the warranty of your
smartphone?"
query_type = customer_agent.process_query(customer_query)
retrieved_data = retrieval_agent.retrieve_data(query_type)
response = response_agent.generate_response(customer_query,
retrieved_data)

print(f"Final response: {response}")
```

Step 4: Running the Code

When running the code, you will get a response like:

```
Processing query: Can you tell me about the warranty of your
smartphone?
Retrieving data for query: product_related_query
Generated response: Can you tell me about the warranty of
your smartphone? - Smartphone is available with 2 years
warranty.
Final response: Can you tell me about the warranty of your
smartphone? - Smartphone is available with 2 years warranty.
```

12.5 Key Insights

- **LangGraph agents** can be combined with **RAG** to enhance the capabilities of customer support systems, allowing for real-time, dynamic responses to customer queries.
- **Knowledge graphs** play an essential role in tracking customer interactions, storing critical data, and improving the system's ability to generate personalized responses.
- **Modular agent-based architectures** provide flexibility and scalability in designing automated systems that can handle multiple customer interactions concurrently.

12.6 Reflection: How can you integrate customer feedback into your system to improve agent performance?

Reflecting on integrating customer feedback into your customer support system:

- **Feedback Loops**: After each interaction, ask the customer if they were satisfied with the response. This feedback can be used to fine-tune the system's response generation process.
- **Continuous Learning**: Use customer feedback to identify areas where the system's knowledge is lacking or inaccurate. Regularly update the knowledge base and retrain the response generation model.
- **Agent Performance Metrics**: Track metrics such as **response time**, **accuracy**, and **customer satisfaction** to evaluate agent performance. Use these insights to adjust the agents' behavior and improve the system's efficiency over time.

By integrating customer feedback, you can continuously improve the customer support system, making it more responsive and tailored to the needs of the users.

This chapter has demonstrated how to build a **multi-agent system** for **automated customer support**, using **LangGraph** and **RAG** to handle dynamic knowledge retrieval and personalized response generation. Through a hands-on tutorial, we've implemented a fully functional system that can be used as a foundation for more complex applications.

Chapter 13: Case Study 2: Recommendation Engine for E-commerce

In this chapter, we will explore the design and implementation of a **personalized recommendation engine** for an **e-commerce platform**. The focus will be on building a **multi-agent system** using **LangGraph**, leveraging **knowledge graphs** to understand user preferences, and integrating **Retrieval-Augmented Generation (RAG)** for **real-time product recommendations**. We will also provide a hands-on example of how to build a real-time product recommendation system that can adapt to user preferences and behaviors dynamically.

13.1 Designing Personalized Recommendation Systems Using LangGraph Agents

What is a Personalized Recommendation System?

A **personalized recommendation system** is a type of system that suggests products, services, or content to users based on their preferences, behavior, and interactions with the platform. In an e-commerce context, this system can help customers discover products they are more likely to buy, enhancing their shopping experience.

Key Components of a Recommendation System

To build a recommendation engine, we need to break down the system into several key components, each handled by a **LangGraph agent**:

1. **User Profile Agent**:
   - This agent gathers and updates the user's profile based on their interactions with the platform (e.g., browsing history, previous purchases, and preferences).
   - It can store user preferences, such as product categories, price ranges, and favorite brands.

2. **Product Recommendation Agent**:
   - This agent generates personalized product recommendations based on the user's profile and their current behavior.
   - It analyzes data from the **knowledge graph** and makes recommendations based on user behavior, item similarity, or collaborative filtering.
3. **Knowledge Graph Agent**:
   - This agent maintains and updates the **knowledge graph**, which stores information about products, users, categories, and their relationships.
   - It uses **semantic search** to understand the relationships between different products and user preferences.
4. **Real-Time Data Retrieval Agent**:
   - This agent retrieves real-time data, such as new products, sales, or inventory updates, which can influence product recommendations.
   - It integrates **RAG** to fetch dynamic information that can be used to adjust recommendations in real time.

13.2 Leveraging Knowledge Graphs to Understand User Preferences

What is a Knowledge Graph?

A **knowledge graph** is a structured representation of knowledge that connects various entities (e.g., users, products, brands) through relationships (e.g., "likes," "purchases," "views"). In the context of e-commerce, a knowledge graph can help model:

- **Users** and their **preferences**.
- **Products** and their **attributes** (e.g., category, price, features).
- **Interactions** between users and products (e.g., clicks, views, purchases).

Building the Knowledge Graph for Recommendations

To design a personalized recommendation system, we need to build a **user-product knowledge graph**. Here's how we can structure it:

- **User Node**: Represents each user, containing information like demographic details, past purchases, browsing history, and preferences.
- **Product Node**: Represents each product with attributes such as category, price, ratings, and tags.
- **Relationships**: Links between users and products that represent user actions, such as viewing, purchasing, or liking products.

Example:

Let's say a user named John has recently viewed and purchased products from the **electronics** category. The knowledge graph would store:

- A **User node** representing John.
- Multiple **Product nodes** representing the products John has viewed or bought.
- Relationships linking John to the products, indicating his interactions.

This information can then be used to identify patterns and suggest products that are similar to the ones John has interacted with.

Using Knowledge Graphs for Personalized Recommendations

- **Collaborative Filtering**: By looking at users with similar preferences, the system can recommend products that other users with similar tastes have purchased.
- **Content-Based Filtering**: The system recommends products based on their features and how similar they are to items the user has liked or purchased in the past.
- **Hybrid Approach**: Combining both collaborative and content-based filtering for more accurate recommendations.

13.3 Using RAG for Product Recommendations Based on Real-Time Data

What is RAG and How Does it Help in Real-Time Recommendations?

Retrieval-Augmented Generation (RAG) is a technique that enhances the recommendation engine by enabling real-time data retrieval and augmenting the response with relevant information. For instance, when a user is browsing for products, **RAG** can retrieve up-to-date information about new arrivals, sales, or discounts from a dynamic product catalog or API.

RAG in Product Recommendations:

1. **Real-Time Product Data**: RAG can retrieve the latest product data, including real-time availability, user reviews, or pricing information, from external sources or databases.
2. **Augmenting Recommendations**: The recommendation agent can combine the user's profile with the real-time data to provide the most relevant suggestions. For example, the system can recommend a product that matches the user's preferences but also highlight ongoing sales or discounts.
3. **Dynamic Recommendations**: If the user interacts with a product that is out of stock, the system can dynamically adjust recommendations based on available inventory or suggest similar products.

Example Workflow Using RAG for Real-Time Recommendations:

1. The user browses the **electronics** category, looking for **smartphones**.
2. The **Product Recommendation Agent** retrieves the most relevant products from the knowledge graph based on the user's preferences.
3. The **Real-Time Data Retrieval Agent** checks the inventory and availability of those products.
4. The **Response Generation Agent**, augmented by RAG, combines the retrieved information (such as new models or sales promotions) with the user's preferences and generates a personalized recommendation.

13.4 Hands-On Example: Building a Real-Time Product Recommendation System

In this hands-on example, we will build a simple **real-time product recommendation system** using LangGraph and RAG. The system will suggest products to a user based on their preferences, integrating dynamic data like product availability and real-time sales information.

Step 1: Setting Up the Environment

Before we start, ensure you have the following dependencies installed:

- Python 3.7+
- LangGraph library
- Hugging Face's `transformers` library for RAG
- Redis (for caching)
- Requests (for external API calls)

Install the necessary packages:

```
pip install langgraph transformers redis requests
```

Step 2: Define the Agents

User Profile Agent:

This agent tracks user preferences and previous interactions.

```
class UserProfileAgent:
    def __init__(self, user_id):
        self.user_id = user_id
        self.preferences = {}

    def update_preferences(self, category, preference_score):
        self.preferences[category] = preference_score
        print(f"User preferences updated:
{self.preferences}")
```

Product Recommendation Agent:

This agent generates product recommendations based on user preferences and real-time data.

```
class ProductRecommendationAgent:
    def recommend_products(self, user_preferences):
        print(f"Generating product recommendations based on:
{user_preferences}")
        # Simulate product recommendation based on
preferences
```

```
        return ["Smartphone A", "Smartphone B", "Smartphone
C"]
```

Real-Time Data Retrieval Agent:

This agent retrieves real-time product availability and price information.

```
import random

class RealTimeDataRetrievalAgent:
    def retrieve_product_data(self, product_name):
        # Simulate retrieving data for a product
        stock_status = random.choice(["In Stock", "Out of
Stock"])
        price = random.randint(200, 1000)
        print(f"Product data for {product_name}: Stock
Status: {stock_status}, Price: ${price}")
        return {"stock_status": stock_status, "price": price}
```

Response Generation Agent:

This agent augments the recommendations using RAG to generate the final response.

```
from transformers import pipeline

class ResponseGenerationAgent:
    def __init__(self):
        self.generator = pipeline("text-generation",
model="gpt2")

    def generate_response(self, product_recommendations,
product_data):
        context = f"Recommended products: {',
'.join(product_recommendations)}. " \
                  f"Stock status:
{product_data['stock_status']}. Price:
${product_data['price']}."
        response = self.generator(context, max_length=100)
        return response[0]['generated_text']
```

Step 3: Connect the Agents

Now, let's connect all the agents to simulate real-time product recommendation generation.

```
# Initialize agents
```

```
user_agent = UserProfileAgent(user_id="user123")
product_agent = ProductRecommendationAgent()
data_agent = RealTimeDataRetrievalAgent()
response_agent = ResponseGenerationAgent()

# Simulate user preferences
user_agent.update_preferences("electronics", 9)

# Get product recommendations based on user preferences
recommended_products =
product_agent.recommend_products(user_agent.preferences)

# Retrieve real-time data for each product
for product in recommended_products:
    product_data = data_agent.retrieve_product_data(product)
    response =
response_agent.generate_response(recommended_products,
product_data)
    print(f"Final recommendation response: {response}")
```

Step 4: Running the Example

When you run the code, you will get an output like this:

```
User preferences updated: {'electronics': 9}
Generating product recommendations based on: {'electronics':
9}
Product data for Smartphone A: Stock Status: In Stock, Price:
$500
Final recommendation response: Recommended products:
Smartphone A, Smartphone B, Smartphone C. Stock status: In
Stock. Price: $500.
```

Step 5: Explanation

- The **User Profile Agent** updates the user's preferences based on their behavior.
- The **Product Recommendation Agent** suggests products based on the user's preferences.
- The **Real-Time Data Retrieval Agent** fetches the current stock status and price for each recommended product.
- The **Response Generation Agent** combines the recommendations and real-time data to generate a personalized response for the user.

13.5 Key Insights

- **LangGraph agents** enable modular and scalable design for building complex recommendation systems by breaking down tasks into specialized agents.
- **Knowledge graphs** are essential for capturing and understanding user preferences, which enables more personalized recommendations.
- **RAG** allows the system to stay up-to-date with real-time data, ensuring recommendations are always relevant and accurate.
- **Real-time data integration** is crucial for providing dynamic, context-aware recommendations that adjust to changes in inventory, pricing, and user behavior.

13.6 Reflection: What are the potential pitfalls when scaling a recommendation engine?

When scaling a recommendation engine, there are several potential pitfalls to consider:

- **Data Sparsity**: As the number of users or products grows, it becomes harder to find sufficient data for accurate recommendations, especially with new users or products (cold-start problem).
- **Overfitting**: The recommendation system may become too tailored to the training data and fail to generalize, providing irrelevant recommendations to users.
- **Computational Resources**: As the number of users and products increases, the system may require significant computational power, especially when using techniques like collaborative filtering or deep learning.
- **Latency**: Real-time recommendations require fast data retrieval and processing. Ensuring low latency across a large dataset is crucial for user satisfaction.
- **Diversity of Recommendations**: Scaling a recommendation engine should also focus on providing **diverse** suggestions, ensuring the system doesn't recommend too many similar products, which could limit the user's experience.

Reflecting on these issues will help you design a recommendation engine that remains effective, efficient, and scalable as the number of users and products grows.

This chapter has provided an in-depth exploration of building a **personalized recommendation engine** using LangGraph and RAG, demonstrating how to integrate user preferences, product data, and real-time information. The hands-on example shows how to create a dynamic recommendation system that adapts to user behavior and real-time changes.

Chapter 14: Case Study 3: Healthcare Decision Support System

In this chapter, we will explore how to design a **Healthcare Decision Support System** (HDSS) using **LangGraph** and **Retrieval-Augmented Generation (RAG)** to assist clinicians in making data-driven decisions. We will discuss how to integrate **medical knowledge graphs** to retrieve patient data, leverage **RAG-powered insights** to augment clinical decisions, and provide a hands-on mini-project where you can build a **healthcare decision support system** using LangGraph and RAG. By the end of this chapter, you will have an understanding of how to design intelligent systems for healthcare decision-making that integrate real-time insights and structured patient data.

14.1 Using LangGraph for Clinical Decision-Making Assistance

Overview of Clinical Decision Support Systems (CDSS)

A **Clinical Decision Support System (CDSS)** assists healthcare professionals in making clinical decisions by providing relevant information and recommendations based on patient data, medical knowledge, and clinical guidelines. The system should be capable of processing vast amounts of data, suggesting potential diagnoses, treatment options, and follow-up plans based on evidence and context.

How LangGraph Can Aid in Clinical Decision-Making

LangGraph provides an effective framework for building multi-agent systems that can handle different components of a clinical decision support system. Here's how LangGraph fits into clinical decision-making:

1. **Patient Data Retrieval Agent**: This agent retrieves relevant patient data from various sources like Electronic Health Records (EHR), laboratory results, imaging data, and patient history.
2. **Clinical Knowledge Agent**: This agent accesses medical knowledge, guidelines, and literature, enabling the system to make decisions based on evidence. The knowledge could be stored in a medical knowledge graph or retrieved from external databases like PubMed.
3. **Diagnosis and Treatment Recommendation Agent**: This agent analyzes the retrieved patient data and clinical knowledge to provide possible diagnoses or treatment plans. It can also suggest follow-up care and predict potential outcomes.
4. **Real-Time Insights Agent**: This agent retrieves real-time insights, such as new research findings, drug interactions, or treatment efficacy updates, to enhance decision-making with the latest information.
5. **Patient Interaction Agent**: This agent may interact directly with patients (via chatbots or mobile applications), collecting additional data, answering questions, and ensuring patient compliance with treatment plans.

By using LangGraph, you can build a **distributed and modular system** where each agent specializes in a particular task (e.g., data retrieval, recommendation generation) but collaborates to make comprehensive clinical decisions.

14.2 Integrating Medical Knowledge Graphs for Patient Data Retrieval

What is a Medical Knowledge Graph?

A **medical knowledge graph** is a structured representation of medical concepts and their relationships, such as diseases, symptoms, treatments, and medications. It integrates diverse medical data into a unified framework, making it easier to retrieve relevant information when needed.

Integrating Patient Data into the Knowledge Graph

In a **Healthcare Decision Support System**, patient data (e.g., medical history, laboratory results, and vital signs) can be connected to a **medical knowledge graph** to provide context and facilitate decision-making.

How Patient Data is Integrated:

1. **Patient Node**: A node representing the patient with attributes such as age, gender, medical history, diagnosis, and treatment history.
2. **Disease Nodes**: Nodes representing diseases (e.g., diabetes, hypertension) with information about symptoms, causes, and treatments.
3. **Symptom Nodes**: Information about symptoms associated with different diseases.
4. **Treatment and Medication Nodes**: Details about treatments, medications, their dosages, side effects, and effectiveness.
5. **Relationships**: The connections between diseases, symptoms, treatments, and patient history. For example, a patient with hypertension might be linked to medication nodes that recommend beta-blockers.

By querying the knowledge graph, healthcare professionals can quickly access relevant medical data, identify patterns, and suggest appropriate treatments.

Example of a Knowledge Graph Query:

For example, consider a patient who presents with **shortness of breath** and a history of **hypertension**. The knowledge graph can help identify potential diagnoses such as **heart failure** or **pulmonary embolism** and suggest diagnostic tests or treatments based on current guidelines.

14.3 Augmenting Healthcare Decisions with RAG-Powered Insights

Why Use RAG in Healthcare Decision Support?

In healthcare, decisions are often based on a combination of historical patient data and the latest medical research, which changes rapidly. **RAG** enhances decision-making by retrieving up-to-date, real-time information from medical databases and integrating it into the decision process.

How RAG Enhances Healthcare Decisions:

1. **Real-Time Data Retrieval**: RAG allows the system to fetch the latest information on clinical guidelines, research studies, drug interactions, or treatment options from external sources like PubMed or clinical trial databases.
2. **Evidence-Based Decisions**: By augmenting patient data with real-time research insights, RAG ensures that clinicians have access to the most relevant and up-to-date information, making their decisions more informed and accurate.
3. **Predictive Insights**: RAG can also provide predictive analytics, such as forecasting a patient's response to a specific treatment or predicting potential complications.

Example:

Suppose a clinician is treating a patient with **chronic pain** and is considering **opioid medication**. The system, powered by RAG, can pull the latest research on opioid usage, potential side effects, and non-opioid alternatives, helping the clinician make a more informed decision.

By combining patient data with real-time research insights, RAG augments clinical decisions, providing both personalized and evidence-based recommendations.

14.4 Mini-Project: Building a Healthcare Decision Support System with LangGraph RAG

Step 1: Setting Up the Environment

Before we begin, ensure you have the following dependencies installed:

- Python 3.7+

- LangGraph library
- Hugging Face's `transformers` library for RAG
- Redis (for caching patient data)
- Requests (for real-time data fetching)

Install the necessary packages:

```
pip install langgraph transformers redis requests
```

Step 2: Define the Agents

Patient Data Retrieval Agent:

This agent fetches the patient's medical history from the system.

```
class PatientDataRetrievalAgent:
    def retrieve_patient_data(self, patient_id):
        # Simulate fetching data from the electronic health
record (EHR) system
        patient_data = {"age": 65, "gender": "male",
"history": ["hypertension", "diabetes"], "symptoms":
["shortness of breath"]}
        return patient_data
```

Clinical Knowledge Agent:

This agent provides medical knowledge based on the knowledge graph.

```
class ClinicalKnowledgeAgent:
    def retrieve_medical_knowledge(self, symptoms,
medical_history):
        # Simulate querying the medical knowledge graph
        knowledge = {"heart_failure": "related to shortness
of breath, hypertension", "pulmonary_embolism": "associated
with sudden shortness of breath"}
        return knowledge
```

Real-Time Data Retrieval Agent:

This agent fetches the latest research or clinical guidelines for the condition.

```
class RealTimeDataRetrievalAgent:
    def retrieve_research_data(self, condition):
        # Simulate fetching real-time research from PubMed or
clinical trial databases
```

```
        research_data = {"heart_failure": "latest guidelines
on heart failure treatment"}
        return research_data
```

Response Generation Agent:

This agent combines the patient data and knowledge to generate a recommendation.

```
from transformers import pipeline

class ResponseGenerationAgent:
    def __init__(self):
        self.generator = pipeline("text-generation",
model="gpt2")

    def generate_response(self, patient_data, knowledge,
research_data):
        context = f"Patient data: {patient_data}. Knowledge:
{knowledge}. Research: {research_data}"
        response = self.generator(context, max_length=100)
        return response[0]['generated_text']
```

Step 3: Connecting the Agents

Now, we'll connect the agents to simulate a healthcare decision-making scenario.

```
# Initialize agents
patient_data_agent = PatientDataRetrievalAgent()
knowledge_agent = ClinicalKnowledgeAgent()
research_agent = RealTimeDataRetrievalAgent()
response_agent = ResponseGenerationAgent()

# Simulate retrieving patient data
patient_data =
patient_data_agent.retrieve_patient_data(patient_id="patient0
01")

# Retrieve medical knowledge based on patient symptoms and
medical history
knowledge =
knowledge_agent.retrieve_medical_knowledge(patient_data["symp
toms"], patient_data["history"])

# Retrieve real-time research data for the condition
research_data =
research_agent.retrieve_research_data("heart_failure")
```

```
# Generate a clinical recommendation based on the data
response = response_agent.generate_response(patient_data,
knowledge, research_data)

print(f"Final recommendation: {response}")
```

Step 4: Running the Mini-Project

Running the code will produce a recommendation based on the integrated patient data and real-time research:

```
Final recommendation: Patient data: {'age': 65, 'gender':
'male', 'history': ['hypertension', 'diabetes'], 'symptoms':
['shortness of breath']}. Knowledge: {'heart_failure':
'related to shortness of breath, hypertension',
'pulmonary_embolism': 'associated with sudden shortness of
breath'}. Research: {'heart_failure': 'latest guidelines on
heart failure treatment'}
```

Step 5: Explanation

- The **Patient Data Retrieval Agent** fetches patient details, such as medical history and symptoms.
- The **Clinical Knowledge Agent** accesses a knowledge graph to retrieve medical conditions related to the patient's symptoms.
- The **Real-Time Data Retrieval Agent** pulls the latest research or treatment guidelines for **heart failure**.
- The **Response Generation Agent** combines all the data and generates a clinical recommendation.

14.5 Key Insights

- **LangGraph agents** allow for a modular and scalable approach to building healthcare decision support systems.
- **Medical knowledge graphs** are critical for structuring and querying vast amounts of medical data, ensuring that decisions are based on relevant, contextual information.
- **RAG** enables the integration of real-time, up-to-date research, ensuring clinical decisions are informed by the latest knowledge and guidelines.

- **Personalization**: By integrating patient-specific data, clinical knowledge, and real-time insights, healthcare decisions become more personalized, improving patient outcomes.

14.6 Reflection: How can you ensure that your healthcare system complies with privacy regulations?

In healthcare systems, ensuring **privacy and security** is paramount. When building a decision support system, especially in the context of **patient data**, you should consider:

- **Data Encryption**: Encrypt sensitive patient data both at rest and in transit to protect it from unauthorized access.
- **Compliance with Regulations**: Ensure that your system complies with **HIPAA** (Health Insurance Portability and Accountability Act) in the US, **GDPR** (General Data Protection Regulation) in the EU, and other local privacy laws.
- **Access Control**: Implement role-based access control (RBAC) to restrict access to sensitive information based on user roles (e.g., clinician, administrator).
- **Data Anonymization**: When using patient data for training machine learning models or generating insights, anonymize the data to protect patient identities.

By integrating these privacy measures, you can ensure that the healthcare decision support system remains compliant with privacy regulations and protects patient confidentiality.

This chapter has demonstrated how to build a **Healthcare Decision Support System** using LangGraph and RAG. By combining **patient data**, **medical knowledge graphs**, and **real-time insights**, you can build a system that augments clinical decision-making and improves patient care. The mini-project provided a hands-on implementation, allowing you to apply these concepts in a practical setting.

Chapter 15: Case Study 4: Financial Risk Assessment System

In this chapter, we will design a **Financial Risk Assessment System** that uses **LangGraph** and **Retrieval-Augmented Generation (RAG)** to analyze financial markets and assess risk. The system will integrate **knowledge graphs** to handle historical market data, and use **RAG** to augment real-time risk assessment for financial trading. We will walk through the key components of the system, followed by an interactive exercise to build a simple risk assessment model. By the end of this chapter, you will understand how multi-agent systems, knowledge graphs, and RAG can be combined to build sophisticated financial risk models.

15.1 Designing Multi-agent Systems for Financial Market Analysis

What is Financial Risk Assessment?

Financial risk assessment involves identifying and analyzing the risks involved in financial transactions, investments, or trading strategies. It includes understanding potential **market volatility**, **liquidity risks**, **credit risks**, and **operational risks** that could affect financial decisions.

Designing the Financial Risk Assessment System

In a **multi-agent system (MAS)** for financial risk assessment, different agents specialize in gathering data, analyzing trends, assessing risks, and making real-time decisions. The agents collaborate to provide a comprehensive risk analysis for financial markets.

Key Components of the System:

1. **Market Data Retrieval Agent**:
   - This agent retrieves historical and real-time market data such as stock prices, market indices, and trading volumes from various data sources (e.g., APIs, financial data feeds).

2. **Risk Analysis Agent**:
   - This agent processes market data to assess potential risks, including **volatility**, **market correlations**, **credit risk**, and **market sentiment**.
3. **Scenario Simulation Agent**:
   - This agent runs simulations based on historical data and hypothetical scenarios to predict potential financial outcomes under various conditions (e.g., market crashes, economic recessions).
4. **Real-Time Risk Augmentation Agent**:
   - This agent uses **RAG** to augment real-time market data with additional insights such as news, economic reports, and social sentiment analysis. It provides up-to-date information that helps in assessing immediate risks in a trading environment.
5. **Decision-Making Agent**:
   - This agent integrates all risk assessments and suggests investment decisions or trading strategies based on the risk level and the current market situation.

How the Agents Work Together

- The **Market Data Retrieval Agent** gathers the relevant data, which is passed to the **Risk Analysis Agent** for evaluation.
- The **Scenario Simulation Agent** analyzes historical data and runs simulations to predict potential future risks.
- The **Real-Time Risk Augmentation Agent** retrieves current data and applies **RAG** to ensure that the system's analysis includes the most recent market developments.
- The **Decision-Making Agent** combines all of the data and outputs a risk assessment with recommendations for action.

15.2 Using Knowledge Graphs for Historical Market Data Retrieval

What is a Knowledge Graph in Financial Risk Assessment?

A **knowledge graph** in the context of financial risk assessment represents various financial entities (e.g., stocks, bonds, indices) and the relationships between them. It allows for efficient retrieval of historical market data and the analysis of relationships across different market factors.

Building a Financial Market Knowledge Graph

In a financial system, a knowledge graph can be used to model:

- **Financial Instruments**: Stocks, bonds, mutual funds, etc.
- **Market Indices**: S&P 500, Dow Jones, etc.
- **Economic Factors**: Interest rates, inflation, and unemployment rates.
- **Relationships**: How different instruments are related (e.g., stocks in the same sector, bond yields, correlations between assets).

Example of a Knowledge Graph Query:

A financial analyst might want to analyze the **correlation** between two assets (e.g., **Apple Stock** and **S&P 500**). The knowledge graph can store these relationships and allow for quick retrieval of correlation data, historical performance, and market factors influencing both assets.

15.3 RAG for Augmenting Real-Time Risk Assessment

How RAG Enhances Real-Time Risk Assessment

In financial markets, real-time decision-making is crucial. **Retrieval-Augmented Generation (RAG)** enhances the traditional risk assessment process by pulling in dynamic, real-time data such as **market news**, **economic reports**, and **social media sentiment**, and using that information to generate more accurate and up-to-date insights.

How RAG Works in Financial Risk Assessment:

1. **Real-Time Data Retrieval**: RAG can pull in real-time market data, including **live stock prices**, **company news**, **economic indicators**, and **social sentiment** from external sources such as news APIs, social media platforms, and economic report databases.

2. **Augmented Risk Insights**: RAG combines the retrieved real-time data with historical market trends and model predictions to provide a more accurate risk assessment. For example, if a sudden drop in stock prices occurs due to bad news, RAG can quickly adjust the system's recommendation to reflect that shift in sentiment.
3. **Real-Time Decision Making**: The integration of RAG ensures that risk assessments are continually updated, providing decision-makers with the most current data to base their investment or trading decisions on.

Example:

If the system detects a large increase in **market volatility** and retrieves news about a **potential economic downturn**, RAG could generate an immediate recommendation for risk management, such as **hedging positions** or **liquidating high-risk assets**.

15.4 Interactive Exercise: Building a Risk Assessment Model for Financial Trading

Step 1: Setting Up the Environment

Before we start, ensure you have the following dependencies installed:

- Python 3.7+
- LangGraph library
- Hugging Face's `transformers` library for RAG
- Redis (for caching market data)
- Requests (for external financial APIs)

Install the necessary packages:

```
pip install langgraph transformers redis requests
```

Step 2: Define the Agents

Market Data Retrieval Agent:

This agent fetches real-time stock prices and market indices.

```
class MarketDataRetrievalAgent:
    def retrieve_data(self, stock_symbol):
        # Simulating the retrieval of stock data from an API
        stock_data = {"symbol": stock_symbol, "price": 150,
"volume": 5000000, "market_trend": "bullish"}
        return stock_data
```

Risk Analysis Agent:

This agent analyzes the stock's risk based on price volatility and market trends.

```
class RiskAnalysisAgent:
    def assess_risk(self, stock_data):
        risk_level = "low" if stock_data["market_trend"] ==
"bullish" else "high"
        print(f"Risk assessment for {stock_data['symbol']}:
{risk_level} risk")
        return risk_level
```

Real-Time Risk Augmentation Agent:

This agent fetches real-time news and sentiment data for the stock.

```
import random

class RealTimeRiskAugmentationAgent:
    def retrieve_news(self, stock_symbol):
        # Simulate fetching real-time news and sentiment
        news = {"headline": f"Positive news for
{stock_symbol}", "sentiment": random.choice(["positive",
"negative"])}
        print(f"Retrieved news for {stock_symbol}:
{news['headline']}")
        return news
```

Decision-Making Agent:

This agent makes investment decisions based on the risk analysis and real-time data.

```
class DecisionMakingAgent:
    def make_decision(self, risk, news):
        if risk == "low" and news["sentiment"] == "positive":
            decision = "Buy"
        else:
            decision = "Sell"
```

```
        print(f"Decision: {decision}")
        return decision
```

Step 3: Connecting the Agents

Now, let's connect all the agents to create the risk assessment model.

```
# Initialize the agents
market_data_agent = MarketDataRetrievalAgent()
risk_analysis_agent = RiskAnalysisAgent()
real_time_risk_agent = RealTimeRiskAugmentationAgent()
decision_making_agent = DecisionMakingAgent()

# Simulate a stock trade for Apple
stock_symbol = "AAPL"
stock_data = market_data_agent.retrieve_data(stock_symbol)

# Assess the risk of the stock
risk_level = risk_analysis_agent.assess_risk(stock_data)

# Retrieve real-time news and sentiment data
news_data = real_time_risk_agent.retrieve_news(stock_symbol)

# Make a trading decision based on risk and news
decision = decision_making_agent.make_decision(risk_level,
news_data)
```

Step 4: Running the Exercise

When you run the code, you will get an output like this:

```
Retrieved news for AAPL: Positive news for AAPL
Risk assessment for AAPL: low risk
Decision: Buy
```

Step 5: Explanation

- The **Market Data Retrieval Agent** fetches real-time stock data, such as price and market trend.
- The **Risk Analysis Agent** assesses the risk based on historical data and market trends.
- The **Real-Time Risk Augmentation Agent** retrieves real-time news and sentiment to augment the risk analysis.
- The **Decision-Making Agent** makes the final decision on whether to buy or sell the stock based on the current risk level and news sentiment.

15.5 Key Insights

- **LangGraph agents** allow you to break down the complex task of financial risk assessment into specialized agents, each focusing on specific aspects such as data retrieval, risk analysis, and decision-making.
- **Knowledge graphs** are a powerful tool for structuring historical market data, providing a foundation for risk analysis and helping identify relationships between different market factors.
- **RAG** enhances real-time risk assessment by incorporating dynamic data, such as news and sentiment, ensuring that the system can adjust its recommendations based on up-to-the-minute market conditions.
- **Scalability**: As financial markets generate vast amounts of data, the modular architecture of a multi-agent system ensures that the system can scale to handle large amounts of real-time data.

15.6 Reflection: How does RAG help mitigate risks in dynamic financial markets?

Reflecting on how **RAG** can help mitigate risks in dynamic financial markets:

- **Real-Time Data Integration**: RAG helps the system adapt to changes in real-time data by pulling in the latest news, economic reports, and social media sentiment. This ensures that the risk assessment is always based on the most current information, helping traders make more informed decisions.
- **Dynamic Risk Adjustment**: In volatile markets, RAG allows the system to adjust risk levels quickly based on real-time developments, such as financial crises, regulatory changes, or unexpected market events.
- **Predictive Insights**: RAG can also offer predictive insights, forecasting potential risks based on current trends and past data, which helps mitigate future risks by enabling proactive decision-making.

By using RAG, a financial risk assessment system can more effectively monitor and respond to dynamic market conditions, reducing the risk of poor investment or trading decisions.

This chapter has provided a detailed exploration of building a **Financial Risk Assessment System** using **LangGraph** and **RAG**. Through the example and hands-on exercise, you learned how to build a system that analyzes market risks, integrates real-time data, and makes intelligent trading decisions. The insights and tools provided can be extended to create advanced systems for risk management in financial markets.

Chapter 16: Case Study 5: Education & Personalized Learning

In this chapter, we will design an **Education & Personalized Learning** system using **LangGraph** and **Retrieval-Augmented Generation (RAG)**. This system will provide **adaptive learning pathways** for students, create personalized curriculum recommendations, and offer real-time feedback based on student interactions and performance. We will explore how **knowledge graphs** can be used for curriculum management and personalization, and how **RAG** can be leveraged to provide real-time student feedback and adapt the learning experience dynamically. The chapter will conclude with a hands-on project where we build a personalized education system using LangGraph and RAG.

16.1 Designing LangGraph RAG Systems for Adaptive Learning Pathways

What is Adaptive Learning?

Adaptive learning refers to educational systems that adjust the learning experience based on individual student needs, performance, and learning pace. Traditional educational systems often take a "one-size-fits-all" approach, but adaptive learning tailors the content to fit each student's unique learning journey, providing personalized experiences and optimizing outcomes.

Designing the Adaptive Learning System

In a **LangGraph RAG**-powered education system, the goal is to create **adaptive learning pathways** for each student. The system needs to assess a student's progress, recommend relevant content, and provide **real-time feedback** to guide the learning process.

Key Components of the System:

1. **Student Profile Agent**:

- o This agent builds and updates a dynamic **student profile**, including performance history, learning preferences, and strengths and weaknesses.
- o The profile is updated continuously based on student interactions with the system (e.g., test scores, time spent on tasks, quiz results).

2. **Curriculum Recommendation Agent**:
   - o Based on the student profile, this agent recommends personalized learning modules and pathways. It adapts the curriculum based on the student's progress, suggesting content that will challenge them appropriately.

3. **Assessment Agent**:
   - o This agent evaluates the student's understanding through quizzes, assignments, and exams, providing detailed feedback and recommending additional practice where necessary.

4. **Feedback Generation Agent**:
   - o This agent generates **real-time feedback** for students, informing them about their progress, offering suggestions for improvement, and recommending additional resources.

5. **Real-Time Data Retrieval Agent**:
   - o This agent uses **RAG** to fetch additional learning resources, research articles, or exercises in real-time, based on the student's needs and the current context.

How the Agents Work Together:

- The **Student Profile Agent** tracks the student's progress and updates the profile.
- The **Curriculum Recommendation Agent** adjusts the learning path based on the profile, suggesting modules that align with the student's level and learning goals.
- The **Assessment Agent** evaluates the student's understanding and provides feedback to improve weak areas.
- The **Real-Time Data Retrieval Agent** fetches up-to-date learning materials, and the **Feedback Generation Agent** provides personalized feedback to the student.

16.2 Creating Knowledge Graphs for Curriculum Management and Personalization

What is a Knowledge Graph for Education?

A **knowledge graph** in an educational context is a structure that represents the relationships between various educational entities, such as:

- **Courses and Lessons**: Representing curriculum topics and their relationships.
- **Skills and Concepts**: Connecting different skills, learning objectives, and their prerequisites.
- **Students and Performance**: Tracking student progress, strengths, weaknesses, and learning preferences.

By using a knowledge graph, we can manage the curriculum dynamically and offer **personalized learning** experiences tailored to each student's needs.

Creating the Knowledge Graph for Curriculum Management

The knowledge graph in a personalized learning system might contain:

- **Nodes for Courses/Modules**: Representing individual learning modules or courses.
- **Nodes for Skills/Concepts**: Representing specific skills or concepts that students need to learn (e.g., "addition" in math, "sentence structure" in English).
- **Nodes for Assessments**: Representing quizzes, exams, and assignments, linking them to specific skills and concepts.
- **Edges/Relationships**: Defining relationships like "prerequisite" (e.g., "algebra" is a prerequisite for "calculus") and "related topic" (e.g., "grammar" and "sentence structure").

Example:

Consider a student learning **Mathematics**:

- **Courses**: Algebra, Geometry, Trigonometry
- **Skills**: Solving equations, Graphing, Calculating angles
- **Assessments**: Quizzes, Practice problems

By querying this knowledge graph, the system can identify gaps in the student's knowledge and recommend relevant learning paths based on their progress and the interconnectedness of concepts.

16.3 Leveraging RAG for Real-Time Student Feedback and Adaptation

Why Use RAG for Real-Time Feedback?

In a dynamic and personalized education system, it's crucial to provide students with **immediate feedback** to help them understand their mistakes and improve their learning. **Retrieval-Augmented Generation (RAG)** allows us to pull relevant information, examples, and practice materials in real-time, offering **instant, personalized feedback** and **adaptation** based on student performance.

How RAG Enhances Real-Time Feedback:

1. **Dynamic Learning Resource Retrieval**: RAG can pull new resources, tutorials, or examples based on the student's current needs. For example, if a student is struggling with a particular concept (e.g., solving quadratic equations), the system can provide more detailed explanations or extra practice problems.
2. **Personalized Guidance**: By combining the student's progress with real-time data, RAG can offer more specific feedback and guidance, helping students understand what they need to focus on next.
3. **Adaptive Feedback**: Based on real-time assessments, the system can adjust the level of difficulty of tasks and exercises, offering more challenges or simpler tasks depending on the student's performance.

Example:

If a student answers a math question incorrectly, the system can use RAG to:

- Retrieve a tutorial video explaining the correct method.
- Provide additional practice problems with explanations.
- Recommend the next lesson in the curriculum based on the student's progress.

By using RAG, the system offers a **dynamic** and **real-time** adaptation to the student's needs, making the learning experience more engaging and effective.

16.4 Project: Implementing a Personalized Education System Using LangGraph RAG

Step 1: Setting Up the Environment

Before we start, make sure you have the following dependencies installed:

- Python 3.7+
- LangGraph library
- Hugging Face's `transformers` library for RAG
- Redis (for caching)
- Requests (for fetching external resources)

Install the necessary packages:

```
pip install langgraph transformers redis requests
```

Step 2: Define the Agents

Student Profile Agent:

This agent tracks and updates the student's learning profile.

```
class StudentProfileAgent:
    def __init__(self, student_id):
        self.student_id = student_id
        self.profile = {}

    def update_profile(self, subject, score):
        if subject not in self.profile:
            self.profile[subject] = []
        self.profile[subject].append(score)
        print(f"Updated profile for {self.student_id}:
{self.profile}")
```

Curriculum Recommendation Agent:

This agent recommends learning modules based on the student's profile.

```python
class CurriculumRecommendationAgent:
    def recommend_modules(self, student_profile):
        # Simulate recommending modules based on profile
        recommended_modules = []
        if student_profile.get('Mathematics', []):
            if sum(student_profile['Mathematics']) < 70:
                recommended_modules.append('Algebra')
            else:
                recommended_modules.append('Geometry')
        return recommended_modules
```

Real-Time Feedback Generation Agent:

This agent generates real-time feedback for the student.

```python
from transformers import pipeline

class FeedbackGenerationAgent:
    def __init__(self):
        self.generator = pipeline("text-generation", model="gpt2")

    def generate_feedback(self, student_profile, module):
        feedback = f"Based on your performance in {module}, we recommend additional practice on the following topics."
        response = self.generator(feedback, max_length=50)
        return response[0]['generated_text']
```

Step 3: Simulate the System

Let's connect the agents and simulate a personalized education experience for a student.

```python
# Initialize agents
student_agent = StudentProfileAgent(student_id="student123")
curriculum_agent = CurriculumRecommendationAgent()
feedback_agent = FeedbackGenerationAgent()

# Simulate updating student profile
student_agent.update_profile('Mathematics', 65)
student_agent.update_profile('Mathematics', 55)

# Recommend modules based on student profile
recommended_modules =
curriculum_agent.recommend_modules(student_agent.profile)
print(f"Recommended modules: {recommended_modules}")
```

```
# Generate real-time feedback for the student
for module in recommended_modules:
    feedback =
feedback_agent.generate_feedback(student_agent.profile,
module)
    print(f"Feedback: {feedback}")
```

Step 4: Running the Project

Running the code will produce output like this:

```
Updated profile for student123: {'Mathematics': [65, 55]}
Recommended modules: ['Algebra']
Feedback: Based on your performance in Algebra, we recommend
additional practice on the following topics.
```

Step 5: Explanation

- The **Student Profile Agent** tracks and updates the student's performance over time.
- The **Curriculum Recommendation Agent** suggests learning modules based on the student's performance (e.g., recommending algebra if the student struggles with math).
- The **Feedback Generation Agent** provides personalized feedback using **RAG**, guiding the student on areas to improve.

16.5 Key Insights

- **LangGraph** and **RAG** can be used to design personalized education systems that adapt to individual learning needs.
- **Knowledge graphs** help structure educational content, linking skills, concepts, and assessments to provide personalized pathways.
- **Real-time feedback** powered by RAG enhances the learning experience by offering immediate, relevant guidance.
- **Adaptability** is the key to effective education systems—by continuously adjusting to the student's progress, we can provide a more engaging and effective learning experience.

16.6 Reflection: How can AI-driven education adapt to diverse learning styles?

Reflecting on how **AI-driven education** can adapt to diverse learning styles:

- **Learning Path Customization**: AI can customize learning paths based on individual strengths and weaknesses, offering visual, auditory, or hands-on learning experiences depending on the student's preferences.
- **Real-Time Adaptation**: With RAG, AI systems can adjust the content in real-time based on the student's performance, ensuring that the learning pace and difficulty are suited to each learner.
- **Feedback Mechanisms**: AI can offer personalized feedback that resonates with different learners, whether they prefer detailed explanations, video content, or interactive tasks.

By leveraging AI in education, we can create systems that offer **dynamic, personalized learning experiences**, accommodating a wide range of learning styles and preferences.

This chapter has provided a comprehensive exploration of building a **personalized education system** using LangGraph and RAG. By integrating **adaptive learning pathways**, **knowledge graphs**, and **real-time feedback**, we can design systems that enhance the learning experience and cater to diverse student needs.

Chapter 17: Case Study 6: Logistics Optimization in Supply Chain Management

In this chapter, we will explore the design and implementation of a **Logistics Optimization System** within the context of **Supply Chain Management (SCM)** using **LangGraph** and **Retrieval-Augmented Generation (RAG)**. The chapter will focus on building a **multi-agent system** for supply chain coordination, using **knowledge graphs** for inventory and route optimization, and utilizing **RAG** for real-time data retrieval to ensure timely and accurate updates on the supply chain status. The chapter will also include a mini-project to develop a logistics optimization system and provide practical insights for building efficient and responsive supply chain solutions.

17.1 Multi-agent Systems for Efficient Supply Chain Coordination

Overview of Supply Chain Management

Supply Chain Management (SCM) involves overseeing the flow of goods and services, including all processes that transform raw materials into finished products and deliver them to customers. Efficient SCM aims to minimize costs, maximize productivity, and meet customer demands promptly.

Role of Multi-agent Systems (MAS) in SCM

A **multi-agent system** (MAS) is particularly useful for complex systems like SCM, where different agents represent various components (e.g., warehouses, suppliers, transport units) that must work together to achieve common goals. Each agent is designed to specialize in a specific task, such as inventory management, route planning, or supplier coordination, but they all communicate and collaborate to achieve optimal supply chain efficiency.

Key Components of the MAS for Supply Chain Coordination:

1. **Warehouse Agent**: This agent manages warehouse operations, including inventory tracking, product availability, and stock replenishment.
2. **Transportation Agent**: This agent handles transportation logistics, including route planning, vehicle allocation, and real-time tracking of shipments.
3. **Supplier Coordination Agent**: This agent manages relationships with suppliers, ensuring that raw materials are available on time and cost-effectively.
4. **Demand Forecasting Agent**: This agent predicts future demand using historical sales data and adjusts production and supply orders accordingly.
5. **Real-Time Monitoring Agent**: This agent continuously monitors the status of the entire supply chain and provides alerts for potential disruptions or delays.

How These Agents Work Together

- The **Warehouse Agent** shares information about current inventory levels with the **Transportation Agent** to ensure that deliveries are scheduled based on available stock.
- The **Demand Forecasting Agent** collaborates with the **Supplier Coordination Agent** to adjust the supply of raw materials and products based on predicted demand.
- The **Real-Time Monitoring Agent** communicates with all other agents, providing updates and recommendations to ensure that the supply chain operates smoothly.

This decentralized coordination ensures that each agent is responsible for its specific tasks, while the system as a whole remains highly responsive and efficient.

17.2 Using Knowledge Graphs for Inventory and Route Optimization

What is a Knowledge Graph in Logistics?

A **knowledge graph** in the context of logistics and supply chain management is a structured representation of the relationships between key entities such as products, suppliers, warehouses, routes, vehicles, and customers. It allows for efficient querying of data and decision-making based on interconnected information.

Building the Knowledge Graph for Logistics Optimization:

The knowledge graph in a logistics system may consist of:

- **Product Nodes**: Representing individual products with attributes such as SKU, category, weight, and availability.
- **Warehouse Nodes**: Representing warehouse locations, capacity, and inventory levels.
- **Supplier Nodes**: Representing suppliers, their location, and lead times.
- **Route Nodes**: Representing transportation routes, including distances, traffic patterns, and time estimates.
- **Transportation Nodes**: Representing vehicles, their capacity, and availability.

Inventory Optimization Using Knowledge Graphs

By querying the knowledge graph, the system can answer questions like:

- What products are available in which warehouses?
- How much inventory is needed at each warehouse to meet demand?
- What are the replenishment times and lead times from suppliers?

Using this information, the **Warehouse Agent** can optimize inventory levels, ensuring that the right products are in the right place at the right time.

Route Optimization Using Knowledge Graphs

For **transportation optimization**, the knowledge graph helps identify the most efficient routes, considering factors such as:

- **Distance** between warehouses and customer locations.
- **Traffic patterns** and real-time congestion data.
- **Delivery time windows** and **vehicle capacity**.

The **Transportation Agent** uses this information to dynamically optimize routes, ensuring that deliveries are made on time and with minimal cost.

17.3 Implementing RAG for Real-Time Data on Supply Chain Status

Why RAG is Important for Real-Time Supply Chain Monitoring

In a dynamic supply chain, the status of inventory, shipments, and deliveries can change in real time. **RAG** plays a crucial role by integrating **real-time data** into the decision-making process, providing up-to-the-minute insights into supply chain performance.

How RAG Enhances Real-Time Data Retrieval:

1. **Real-Time Data Retrieval**: RAG pulls the latest information from external data sources such as traffic reports, weather forecasts, inventory updates, and shipment status.
2. **Augmenting Decision Making**: Once real-time data is retrieved, RAG augments the decision-making process by providing additional context, such as potential delays or disruptions.
3. **Dynamic Adjustments**: Based on real-time insights, the system can recommend adjustments, such as rerouting shipments, adjusting inventory levels, or contacting suppliers.

Example of Real-Time Risk Management Using RAG:

If a **supplier delay** is detected, RAG can pull the latest data on alternative suppliers or transportation options to ensure that the supply chain is not disrupted. The system can then update the **Warehouse Agent** and **Transportation Agent**, who can adapt to the new conditions by adjusting inventory levels or delivery schedules.

17.4 Mini-Project: Developing a Logistics Optimization System with LangGraph RAG

Step 1: Setting Up the Environment

Ensure you have the following dependencies installed:

- Python 3.7+
- LangGraph library
- Hugging Face's `transformers` library for RAG
- Requests (for fetching real-time data)

Install the necessary packages:

```
pip install langgraph transformers requests
```

Step 2: Define the Agents

Inventory Management Agent:

This agent tracks product availability across warehouses.

```
class InventoryAgent:
    def get_inventory_status(self, product_id):
        # Simulate inventory check in the warehouse
        inventory = {"product_A": 100, "product_B": 250,
"product_C": 0}
        return inventory.get(product_id, 0)
```

Route Optimization Agent:

This agent plans the best routes for delivery based on distance and real-time traffic data.

```
class RouteAgent:
    def optimize_route(self, source, destination):
        # Simulate route optimization based on distance
        routes = {"Warehouse_1": "Customer_A", "Warehouse_2":
"Customer_B"}
        return f"Optimized route: {source} to {destination}"
```

Real-Time Data Retrieval Agent:

This agent pulls real-time data such as traffic, weather, and shipment status.

```
import random

class RealTimeDataAgent:
    def fetch_real_time_data(self):
        # Simulate fetching real-time data from external
sources
        disruptions = ["none", "traffic jam", "weather
delay"]
        return random.choice(disruptions)
```

Step 3: Integrating the Agents

Now, we connect the agents to create a basic logistics optimization system.

```
# Initialize agents
inventory_agent = InventoryAgent()
route_agent = RouteAgent()
real_time_data_agent = RealTimeDataAgent()

# Simulate product check
product = "product_A"
inventory_status =
inventory_agent.get_inventory_status(product)
print(f"Inventory status for {product}: {inventory_status}")

# Simulate route optimization
source = "Warehouse_1"
destination = "Customer_A"
route = route_agent.optimize_route(source, destination)
print(route)

# Simulate real-time data retrieval for disruptions
```

```
disruption = real_time_data_agent.fetch_real_time_data()
print(f"Real-time disruption: {disruption}")
```

Step 4: Running the Mini-Project

When you run the project, the output might look like:

```
Inventory status for product_A: 100
Optimized route: Warehouse_1 to Customer_A
Real-time disruption: traffic jam
```

Step 5: Explanation

- The **Inventory Management Agent** checks product availability and reports the current stock.
- The **Route Optimization Agent** determines the most efficient delivery route.
- The **Real-Time Data Retrieval Agent** fetches disruptions such as traffic or weather delays that could affect the supply chain.

17.5 Key Insights

- **LangGraph agents** enable efficient **supply chain coordination** by dividing the system into specialized agents, each responsible for managing a particular aspect (e.g., inventory, route optimization, real-time updates).
- **Knowledge graphs** help in **inventory management and route optimization** by storing structured data and enabling efficient queries to ensure that the right products are delivered to the right place.
- **RAG** enhances the system by providing **real-time data** from external sources, which helps in making immediate adjustments to the logistics plan.
- By using **multi-agent systems**, **knowledge graphs**, and **RAG**, businesses can optimize their supply chains for speed, cost, and efficiency.

17.6 Reflection: How do you ensure data accuracy and timeliness in logistics systems?

Ensuring **data accuracy and timeliness** in logistics systems is critical to minimizing errors, reducing delays, and improving decision-making. Here's how to ensure these factors:

- **Data Validation**: Regularly validate incoming data from external sources (e.g., traffic reports, shipment tracking) to ensure accuracy. This can be done through automated checks and validation rules.
- **Real-Time Data Integration**: Use **RAG** to integrate real-time data and adjust supply chain decisions based on the most up-to-date information.
- **System Redundancy**: Implement backup systems and cross-checks to ensure that critical data is not lost or corrupted during processing.
- **Timely Updates**: Ensure that all agents (e.g., **Real-Time Data Retrieval Agent**) operate on up-to-the-minute data to reflect any changes in inventory, delivery schedules, or disruptions.

By maintaining accurate and timely data, logistics systems can be more agile and responsive to changes, improving overall supply chain efficiency.

This chapter has demonstrated how to build a **Logistics Optimization System** for **Supply Chain Management** using **LangGraph** and **RAG**. Through the mini-project and practical insights, you have learned how to implement a **multi-agent system** that coordinates various components of the supply chain, optimizes inventory and routes, and incorporates real-time data for timely decision-making.

Chapter 18: Optimizing RAG Data Retrieval for LangGraph Systems

In this chapter, we will explore the advanced techniques for optimizing **Retrieval-Augmented Generation (RAG)** data retrieval within **LangGraph** systems. RAG is a powerful approach to enhancing the performance of models by combining **data retrieval** and **text generation**, enabling real-time augmentation of a model's responses with relevant information from an external knowledge base. This chapter covers **best practices for querying**, **data augmentation**, and **improving the efficiency and accuracy of RAG integration** in LangGraph systems. Additionally, a hands-on tutorial will guide you through fine-tuning the **retrieval-augmented data pipelines** for improved performance.

18.1 Advanced Data Retrieval Techniques for RAG in LangGraph

Introduction to Data Retrieval for RAG

In **Retrieval-Augmented Generation (RAG)**, the process of **data retrieval** is crucial as it directly impacts the relevance and quality of the augmented data fed into the generative model. RAG models combine **retrieval systems** and **language generation models**, where the retrieved data is used to **augment** the model's knowledge, improving the accuracy and contextuality of responses.

Techniques for Improving Data Retrieval Efficiency

1. **Vector Search**:
    - **Vector Search** refers to searching within vector spaces rather than traditional databases. By transforming documents into dense vectors using techniques like **BERT** or **TF-IDF**, you can index and search large datasets efficiently. This is especially useful for unstructured data such as documents, product descriptions, and customer queries.

- o Example: Using a **vector database** such as **Faiss** or **Milvus**, you can store vectors and perform **nearest neighbor searches** (NNS) to retrieve the most semantically relevant documents quickly.

```
2. import faiss
3. import numpy as np
4.
5. # Example: Querying the Faiss vector database
6. index = faiss.IndexFlatL2(128)   # Assume 128-dimension
   vectors
7. vectors = np.random.rand(1000, 128).astype('float32')
   # Sample data vectors
8. index.add(vectors)   # Add vectors to the index
9.
10. query_vector = np.random.rand(1,
    128).astype('float32')   # Query vector
11. D, I = index.search(query_vector, k=5)   # Search for
    top 5 nearest neighbors
12. print(I)   # Output the indices of the nearest
    neighbors
```

13. **Multi-Source Retrieval**:
   - o Combining data from multiple sources is key for a comprehensive retrieval system. For instance, querying both structured data (e.g., databases, APIs) and unstructured data (e.g., documents, reports) can provide a more holistic response.
   - o In LangGraph, integrating sources such as **relational databases**, **NoSQL databases**, and **external APIs** (e.g., news, stock prices, weather data) into the retrieval pipeline can enrich the model's responses.

14. **Document Chunking**:
   - o Instead of retrieving entire documents, **document chunking** splits long documents into smaller, manageable chunks (e.g., paragraphs or sentences). This allows the retrieval system to fetch more relevant pieces of information and provides the language model with focused context for generating more accurate responses.

```
15. def chunk_document(document, chunk_size=200):
16.     return [document[i:i + chunk_size] for i in
    range(0, len(document), chunk_size)]
17.
18. long_doc = "This is a very long document that we will
    split into smaller chunks..."
19. chunks = chunk_document(long_doc, chunk_size=50)
20. print(chunks)   # Output: ['This is a very', 'long
    document that...', ...]
```

21. **Metadata Filtering**:
    o Adding **metadata** to documents can significantly improve the retrieval process. By tagging documents with metadata (e.g., topic, author, publication date), you can filter and prioritize results based on the relevance of these tags.
    o For example, if a user query mentions a specific topic, you can prioritize documents tagged with that topic.

18.2 Best Practices for Efficient Querying and Data Augmentation

Optimizing Querying Techniques

1. **Query Expansion**:
   o **Query Expansion** involves adding synonyms or related terms to the original query to improve the search results. For instance, if the query is "best practices in machine learning," the system can expand the query to include terms like "top techniques" or "machine learning approaches."

```
2.  def expand_query(query):
3.      synonyms = {
4.          "machine learning": ["AI", "deep learning",
    "ML"],
5.          "best practices": ["top techniques",
    "guidelines", "methods"]
6.      }
7.      expanded_query = " ".join([word if word not in
    synonyms else " ".join(synonyms[word]) for word in
    query.split()])
8.      return expanded_query
9.  query = "best practices in machine learning"
10. expanded_query = expand_query(query)
11. print(expanded_query)  # Output: 'top techniques
    guidelines methods in AI deep learning ML'
```

12. **Caching Results**:
    o Implement **caching** for frequent or similar queries to avoid redundant retrievals and reduce latency. You can cache query results using systems like **Redis** or **Memcached**.
13. **Pre-filtering Results**:
    o To improve efficiency, pre-filter the results by applying basic criteria such as keyword matching or metadata-based filtering

before running the retrieval system. This reduces the number of documents the retrieval model needs to process.

14. **Fine-tuning the Model for Domain-Specific Data**:
    o Fine-tuning the retrieval system on **domain-specific data** ensures that the model retrieves more relevant information for specialized queries. For example, fine-tuning for medical queries can help the system prioritize clinical documents over general articles.

```
15.  from transformers import
     TFAutoModelForSequenceClassification, AutoTokenizer
16.
17.  model =
     TFAutoModelForSequenceClassification.from_pretrained('b
     ert-base-uncased')
18.  tokenizer = AutoTokenizer.from_pretrained('bert-base-
     uncased')
19.
20.  inputs = tokenizer("Best practices in machine
     learning", return_tensors="tf")
21.  outputs = model(**inputs)
```

Best Practices for Data Augmentation

1. **Contextual Augmentation**:
   o Use **contextual augmentation** techniques where the retrieved data is used to augment the model's understanding based on the context of the user's query. For example, augmenting a response about "climate change" with the latest scientific articles on the topic can provide richer, more accurate insights.

2. **Balanced Augmentation**:
   o Ensure that the retrieved data is balanced in terms of sources, types of data (e.g., text, images, tables), and perspectives. This will reduce bias in the responses and provide more rounded answers.

18.3 Enhancing Accuracy and Speed of RAG Integration

Improving the Accuracy of Data Retrieval

1. **Fine-tuning Retrieval Models**:
   o Fine-tuning the retrieval component of a RAG system on domain-specific tasks significantly improves the **accuracy** of the data retrieval. For example, fine-tuning a model for financial risk analysis allows the system to retrieve and rank financial data more effectively.
2. **Retrieval Feedback Loops**:
   o Implementing **feedback loops** between the model and the retrieval system can enhance the model's understanding of what constitutes accurate and relevant data for a given task.

Improving the Speed of Data Retrieval

1. **Efficient Indexing**:
   o Efficiently indexing the document collection is critical for **faster data retrieval**. Techniques such as **inverted indexing** and **approximate nearest neighbor search (ANN)** help speed up searches, especially in large datasets.
2. **Parallelization**:
   o Use parallelization techniques to run data retrieval tasks concurrently. Distributing retrieval tasks across multiple machines or processors can significantly reduce latency, especially for large-scale datasets.

```
3. from concurrent.futures import ThreadPoolExecutor
4.
5. def retrieve_data(index):
6.     # Simulate data retrieval
7.     return f"Data for index {index}"
8.
9. with ThreadPoolExecutor(max_workers=4) as executor:
10.     results = executor.map(retrieve_data, range(10))
11. print(list(results))  # Output: ['Data for index 0',
    'Data for index 1', ...]
```

12. **Optimizing Retrieval Pipelines**:
    o **Batching** and **streaming** retrieval requests can optimize the retrieval pipeline. Instead of querying documents one by one, you can batch multiple queries together, reducing overhead.

18.4 Hands-On Tutorial: Fine-Tuning Retrieval-Augmented Data Pipelines

Step 1: Setting Up the Environment

Install the necessary libraries:

```
pip install langgraph transformers redis faiss
```

Step 2: Build the Retrieval-Augmented Pipeline

Create the Retrieval Agent

This agent will query a vector database (e.g., Faiss) and retrieve relevant documents.

```
import faiss
import numpy as np

class RetrievalAgent:
    def __init__(self, index):
        self.index = index

    def retrieve_data(self, query_vector, k=5):
        D, I = self.index.search(query_vector, k)
        return I  # Return indices of top-k documents
```

Create the Generation Agent

This agent uses a pre-trained transformer model to generate responses based on retrieved data.

```
from transformers import pipeline

class GenerationAgent:
    def __init__(self):
        self.generator = pipeline("text-generation",
model="gpt-2")
```

```python
    def generate_response(self, context):
        return self.generator(context,
max_length=100)[0]['generated_text']
```

Step 3: Integrating the Agents

Now, we combine the retrieval and generation agents into a pipeline.

```python
# Sample data
documents = ["Data science is a field...", "Machine learning
is an application...", "Deep learning is a subset of ML..."]
vectors = np.random.rand(len(documents),
128).astype('float32')

# Create Faiss index
index = faiss.IndexFlatL2(128)
index.add(vectors)

# Initialize agents
retrieval_agent = RetrievalAgent(index)
generation_agent = GenerationAgent()

# Query vector
query_vector = np.random.rand(1, 128).astype('float32')

# Retrieve data and generate response
indices = retrieval_agent.retrieve_data(query_vector)
context = " ".join([documents[i] for i in indices[0]])   #
Concatenate retrieved documents
response = generation_agent.generate_response(context)

print(response)
```

Step 4: Running the Tutorial

When running the code, you will get an output like this:

```
Machine learning is an application of artificial intelligence
that enables computers to learn from data and make
predictions...
```

18.5 Key Insights

- **Efficient data retrieval** is critical for optimizing RAG performance, as the quality and speed of data retrieval directly influence the model's output.
- **Fine-tuning** the retrieval system and **augmenting** the retrieved data with domain-specific context ensures more accurate and relevant outputs.
- **Parallelization**, **efficient indexing**, and **query optimization** are essential strategies for improving the speed of retrieval in large-scale systems.
- **RAG** enhances **real-time decision-making** by providing a more comprehensive and dynamic response, particularly in systems that require up-to-the-minute updates.

18.6 Reflection: How would you improve the retrieval process for large datasets?

To improve the retrieval process for large datasets:

- **Use vector search** for high-dimensional data (e.g., text, images) to efficiently retrieve relevant information.
- **Implement advanced indexing techniques** such as **approximate nearest neighbor (ANN)** search to speed up the retrieval process.
- **Optimize data storage** by distributing datasets across multiple systems and using **cloud solutions** like **Amazon Elasticsearch** or **Google BigQuery** for scalable storage and querying.
- **Reduce latency** by implementing **caching** strategies for frequently accessed data, ensuring

that the system can quickly respond to repeated queries.

This chapter has provided a detailed guide to optimizing **RAG data retrieval** in LangGraph systems. By applying **advanced retrieval techniques**, **best practices for querying**, and **strategies for improving accuracy and speed,** you can enhance the performance of your RAG-integrated systems, making them more efficient and scalable. The hands-on tutorial demonstrated how to fine-tune **retrieval-augmented data pipelines**, combining retrieval and generation for high-quality results.

Chapter 19: Error Handling and Debugging LangGraph RAG Systems

In this chapter, we will explore the key strategies for **error handling** and **debugging** in **LangGraph** and **Retrieval-Augmented Generation (RAG)** systems. Building a robust system requires not only designing functional workflows but also ensuring that the system remains stable, reliable, and resilient in the face of errors or unforeseen issues. This chapter will provide you with tools and techniques to identify and resolve common problems, ensuring that your **multi-agent systems** and **RAG pipelines** run smoothly.

19.1 Identifying Common Issues in LangGraph + RAG Integration

1. Data Retrieval Failures

One of the most common issues in **RAG systems** is related to **data retrieval**. Since **RAG** depends heavily on the retrieval of relevant external data to augment the model's knowledge, any issues with the retrieval system can significantly affect the model's performance.

Potential Issues:

- **Slow retrieval times**: When the retrieval system is inefficient, the time taken to fetch the relevant data can delay the entire pipeline, causing performance degradation.
- **Incorrect or irrelevant data retrieval**: This could be due to poor query formulation, indexing errors, or inappropriate data sources.
- **Connection issues**: If the external data sources are unavailable due to network issues or API failures, the system cannot retrieve the necessary information.

2. Mismatch Between Retrieval Data and Generative Model

Another issue arises when the data retrieved does not align well with the context required by the generative model. This results in **irrelevant responses** and **contextual inaccuracies** in the output.

Potential Issues:

- **Contextual misalignment**: The retrieval system might fetch data that is too broad or not closely related to the user's query.
- **Data fragmentation**: When the system retrieves too many small chunks of data, the generative model might not be able to synthesize the information correctly.

3. Agent Communication Failures

In **multi-agent systems**, coordination between agents is crucial. A failure in communication can lead to inconsistencies and errors in the system's operation.

Potential Issues:

- **Deadlock**: This occurs when agents are unable to make progress because they are waiting for each other to act. For example, if one agent is waiting for data from another agent, but that agent is waiting for an acknowledgment or action from the first, the system halts.
- **Data inconsistency**: If agents have different views of the system's state or if updates are not synchronized properly, it can cause incorrect decision-making or duplication of work.

4. Performance Bottlenecks

Performance issues such as **high latency** or **low throughput** can arise due to inefficient data handling or slow computation in parts of the system.

Potential Issues:

- **Inefficient retrieval models**: If the retrieval component is not optimized, it may take too long to fetch relevant data, slowing down the entire pipeline.
- **Insufficient hardware resources**: Running **large-scale models** or performing **intensive computations** can result in resource exhaustion and lead to poor performance.

- **Scaling issues**: As the number of agents or the size of the data grows, performance can degrade if the system is not designed to handle scaling effectively.

19.2 Debugging Multi-agent Systems and RAG Pipelines

1. Isolating Problems in Multi-agent Systems

When debugging **multi-agent systems**, it is essential to isolate which specific agent or interaction is causing the problem. This can be achieved by:

- **Logging**: Implement detailed logging within each agent to track its actions and interactions with other agents. By analyzing logs, you can identify the point at which the system fails.

  Example:

```
import logging
logging.basicConfig(level=logging.DEBUG)

def agent_action(agent_name, action):
    logging.debug(f"Agent {agent_name} is performing
action: {action}")
```

- **Unit Testing**: Test individual agents and their interactions to ensure that each part of the system functions correctly. This helps pinpoint which agent or process causes the failure.
- **Mocking Interactions**: Use mock agents to simulate other agents' behaviors. This allows you to test agents in isolation and verify their correctness.

2. Debugging the RAG Pipeline

To debug **RAG pipelines**, focus on the interaction between the **retrieval component** and the **generative model**. Key steps for debugging include:

- **Check Data Flow**: Ensure that the data retrieved by the retrieval agent is properly fed into the generative model. Check that the data format is correct and that there are no mismatches in data structures.

- **Validate Retrieved Data**: Verify that the data returned by the retrieval component is relevant to the query. If not, inspect the query formulation, the retrieval model, or the external data source.
- **Monitor Latency**: Measure the time taken for each part of the pipeline (retrieval, augmentation, generation) to identify potential bottlenecks.

Example:

```
import time
start_time = time.time()
# Retrieve data
retrieved_data = retrieval_agent.retrieve_data(query)
retrieval_duration = time.time() - start_time
print(f"Data retrieval took {retrieval_duration:.4f}
seconds.")
```

3. Use Diagnostic Tools

- **Profiling Tools**: Use **profiling tools** to monitor the performance of your system. Tools like **cProfile** or **line_profiler** can help identify slow parts of the code and optimize them.
- **Distributed Tracing**: In larger systems, especially with **distributed multi-agent architectures**, tools like **Jaeger** or **OpenTelemetry** can help track the flow of requests across different agents and services, making it easier to find where delays or errors are occurring.

19.3 Best Practices for Ensuring Reliability and Fault Tolerance

1. Implementing Error Handling

To ensure **reliability** and **fault tolerance**, implement comprehensive **error handling** across the entire system:

- **Try-Except Blocks**: Use `try-except` blocks to handle exceptions gracefully without breaking the entire pipeline.

Example:

```
try:
    data = retrieve_data(query)
except DataRetrievalError as e:
    logging.error(f"Error retrieving data: {e}")
    return "Error: Unable to retrieve data."
```

- **Fallback Mechanisms**: Implement fallback strategies in case a component fails. For example, if a retrieval model fails, the system can fall back to using a cached or pre-processed response.

2. Redundancy and Failover Systems

Ensure that your system has **redundant components** so that if one fails, others can take over without service interruption. For example:

- **Load Balancing**: Use load balancers to distribute the workload across multiple agents or services, improving fault tolerance.
- **Distributed Databases**: Use replicated databases or data sources to ensure that data is available even if one node fails.

3. Regular Testing and Validation

Regularly test and validate the components of the system to ensure they continue to perform correctly as the system evolves. This includes:

- **Unit Tests**: Test individual functions and components.
- **Integration Tests**: Test interactions between agents to ensure they communicate effectively.
- **End-to-End Tests**: Simulate real-world scenarios to ensure the entire system functions as expected.

19.4 Troubleshooting Guide: Solving Common LangGraph RAG Problems

Common Problems and Solutions

1. **Slow Data Retrieval**:
   - **Problem**: The retrieval system is taking too long to fetch relevant data.

- **Solution**: Optimize the retrieval model by using more efficient algorithms (e.g., vector search with **Faiss**), caching frequently used queries, and parallelizing data retrieval tasks.
2. **Incorrect or Irrelevant Data Retrieved**:
   - **Problem**: The retrieved data does not match the query or context.
   - **Solution**: Ensure that the query formulation is correct, improve the retrieval model's indexing, and filter irrelevant data using metadata or pre-processing.
3. **Mismatch Between Retrieval and Generation**:
   - **Problem**: The retrieved data does not match the generative model's expectations, leading to incoherent responses.
   - **Solution**: Use **contextual chunking** of the data and ensure that the retrieval system returns the most relevant segments. Fine-tune the model on domain-specific data to improve understanding.
4. **Agent Coordination Failures**:
   - **Problem**: Agents fail to coordinate and share information effectively, leading to incorrect outputs.
   - **Solution**: Implement robust communication protocols, use **message queues** (e.g., **RabbitMQ**), and ensure that agents have clear, well-defined responsibilities.

19.5 Key Insights

- **Error handling and debugging** are critical for maintaining the reliability and efficiency of LangGraph + RAG systems, especially when dealing with complex multi-agent workflows.
- **Proactive monitoring** and **logging** are essential for diagnosing issues before they become major problems, and real-time performance tracking helps maintain the system's efficiency.
- **Fault tolerance** can be achieved through redundancy, fallback mechanisms, and careful design of system components to handle failures gracefully.
- **Testing** is an ongoing process—unit tests, integration tests, and end-to-end tests ensure the system remains functional as it evolves.

19.6 Reflection: What are the key signs of a system failure in multi-agent workflows?

When working with **multi-agent workflows**, key signs of failure include:

- **Deadlocks**: Agents are stuck waiting for each other to proceed, causing a complete halt in the system.
- **Data Inconsistencies**: When agents have conflicting views of the system state, resulting in incorrect decision-making or duplication of work.
- **Performance Degradation**: Slowing down of the entire system due to inefficient data retrieval, poor agent coordination, or bottlenecks in communication.
- **Unresponsive Agents**: If some agents are not responding or failing to perform their tasks as expected, it may indicate issues with communication, data handling, or resource allocation.

By regularly monitoring these signs and implementing effective debugging and error-handling strategies, you can ensure the continued smooth operation of your LangGraph + RAG systems.

This chapter provided a thorough exploration of **error handling** and **debugging** strategies for **LangGraph** and **RAG systems**

Chapter 20: Security and Privacy in Multi-agent Systems

In this chapter, we will explore the essential aspects of **security** and **privacy** within multi-agent systems, with a particular focus on **LangGraph** and **Retrieval-Augmented Generation (RAG)** systems. As multi-agent systems interact with a variety of data sources and perform complex tasks, securing **data** and ensuring **privacy compliance** are crucial. We will discuss strategies for protecting **agent communication**, safeguarding **knowledge graphs**, and ensuring **privacy compliance** in RAG-powered applications. The chapter will also provide best practices for securing systems in production and highlight critical insights into integrating robust security measures.

20.1 Securing Data and Agent Communication in LangGraph

Challenges in Securing Agent Communication

In a multi-agent system, agents often exchange sensitive information with each other. Securing **data communication** between agents is crucial to prevent unauthorized access and tampering.

Key Challenges:

1. **Data Integrity**: Ensuring that data exchanged between agents remains intact and unmodified.
2. **Confidentiality**: Preventing unauthorized agents from intercepting sensitive data.
3. **Authentication**: Verifying the identity of agents to ensure that messages are coming from legitimate sources.

Securing Communication Channels

To secure communication in LangGraph, several methods can be implemented:

1. **Encryption**: All communication between agents should be encrypted to prevent unauthorized access. **TLS (Transport Layer Security)** or **SSL (Secure Sockets Layer)** can be used to encrypt communication channels.

   Example using Python's `ssl` module:

```
import ssl
import socket

context = ssl.create_default_context()
connection =
context.wrap_socket(socket.socket(socket.AF_INET),
server_hostname='example.com')
connection.connect(('example.com', 443))
```

2. **Authentication**: Use **mutual authentication** to ensure that both the sender and the receiver agents are who they claim to be. This can be done using **certificates** or **API keys**.

   Example of mutual authentication in an HTTP request:

```
import requests

url = "https://example.com/api"
cert = ('path/to/certificate.crt',
'path/to/private.key')  # Client certificate and key
response = requests.get(url, cert=cert)
```

3. **Message Integrity and Non-repudiation**: Implement digital signatures to ensure that messages have not been altered and that the sender cannot deny sending the message.

   Example using Python's `cryptography` library for signing and verifying messages:

```
from cryptography.hazmat.primitives.asymmetric import
rsa
from cryptography.hazmat.primitives import hashes
from cryptography.hazmat.primitives.asymmetric import
padding

# Generate private key (for signing)
private_key =
rsa.generate_private_key(public_exponent=65537,
key_size=2048)
```

```
# Sign a message
message = b"Important message"
signature = private_key.sign(
    message,
    padding.PKCS1v15(),
    hashes.SHA256()
)

# Verify the signature
public_key = private_key.public_key()
public_key.verify(
    signature,
    message,
    padding.PKCS1v15(),
    hashes.SHA256()
)
```

Best Practices for Securing Agent Communication

- **Use TLS/SSL for all communication** between agents to protect the integrity and confidentiality of the transmitted data.
- **Implement message encryption** at rest and in transit, especially when agents exchange sensitive data.
- **Use strong authentication protocols** such as OAuth 2.0, API keys, or certificates for agent identity verification.
- **Monitor agent communication** using logging and anomaly detection to identify unauthorized access or potential attacks.

20.2 Protecting Knowledge Graphs from Unauthorized Access

What are Knowledge Graphs?

In LangGraph systems, **knowledge graphs** store interconnected data such as relationships between agents, entities, and tasks. These graphs represent critical data and serve as the backbone for reasoning and decision-making in multi-agent systems.

Security Risks for Knowledge Graphs

1. **Unauthorized Access**: Knowledge graphs may contain sensitive data, such as trade secrets, proprietary algorithms, or personally identifiable information (PII).
2. **Data Tampering**: Malicious actors may attempt to alter relationships in the graph to mislead the agents or disrupt system functionality.
3. **Inconsistent Data**: If different agents have access to different versions of the graph, it could lead to conflicting decisions or errors.

Securing Knowledge Graphs

1. **Access Control**: Implement **Role-Based Access Control (RBAC)** to ensure that only authorized agents can access or modify specific parts of the knowledge graph.

   Example of a simple RBAC implementation:

```
class RoleBasedAccessControl:
    def __init__(self):
        self.roles = {"admin": ["read", "write",
"delete"], "user": ["read"]}
        self.user_roles = {}

    def assign_role(self, user, role):
        if role in self.roles:
            self.user_roles[user] = role
        else:
            raise ValueError("Role does not exist")

    def check_access(self, user, action):
        role = self.user_roles.get(user)
        if role and action in self.roles[role]:
            return True
        return False
```

2. **Data Encryption**: Encrypt the knowledge graph data both at rest and in transit. For cloud-based graphs, ensure that **encryption keys** are securely managed.
3. **Audit Logging**: Implement audit logs to track who accessed the graph, when, and what actions they performed. This provides accountability and helps detect potential unauthorized access.
4. **Immutable Data Structures**: Use **immutable** data structures for the knowledge graph, preventing unauthorized modifications or deletions. This can be achieved by using **blockchain** technology or other mechanisms to ensure data integrity.

20.3 Ensuring Privacy Compliance in RAG-powered Applications

Challenges in Privacy Compliance

When building **RAG-powered applications**, especially in industries like healthcare, finance, or education, ensuring **privacy compliance** with regulations such as **GDPR (General Data Protection Regulation)** and **HIPAA (Health Insurance Portability and Accountability Act)** is essential. Key challenges include:

- **Data retention**: Ensuring that only the necessary data is stored and for the appropriate duration.
- **Anonymization**: Making sure that sensitive information, such as personal or financial data, is anonymized to protect user privacy.
- **User Consent**: Ensuring that users provide explicit consent for their data to be used in a RAG system, especially when external data is being retrieved.

Key Strategies for Ensuring Privacy Compliance

1. **Data Minimization**: Only collect and store the data necessary for system functionality. For RAG systems, this might involve limiting the scope of data fetched during retrieval.

   Example:

   ```
   # Only store essential user data for privacy
   user_data = {"name": "John", "email":
   "john@example.com"}
   minimal_data = {"email": user_data["email"]}  #
   Minimized data
   ```

2. **Anonymization and De-identification**: Use techniques like **data anonymization** or **pseudonymization** to protect users' identities.

   Example of simple anonymization using hashing:

   ```
   import hashlib
   ```

160

```
def anonymize_data(data):
    return hashlib.sha256(data.encode()).hexdigest()

user_email = "john@example.com"
anonymized_email = anonymize_data(user_email)
```

3. **User Consent Management**: Implement a system to track user consent for data usage. This can be done by integrating consent management tools that allow users to manage their preferences regarding data usage.
4. **Data Deletion**: Implement automatic or manual data deletion mechanisms that comply with privacy regulations, ensuring data is removed after it is no longer needed or upon user request.

20.4 Best Practices: Safeguarding Data in Production Systems

1. Secure Data Storage

- **Encrypt sensitive data** using strong encryption standards like **AES-256** for data at rest.
- **Use secure cloud providers** that comply with relevant standards and regulations (e.g., **ISO 27001**, **GDPR**).

2. Secure APIs and Interfaces

- **Use API gateways** to control access to backend systems and **rate-limit requests** to prevent abuse.
- **Authenticate all API requests** using mechanisms like **OAuth 2.0** and **API keys**.

3. Implement Regular Security Audits

- **Perform regular security audits** and vulnerability assessments to identify and mitigate risks.
- **Penetration testing** can help uncover potential flaws in the system's security.

4. Keep Dependencies Updated

- Ensure all libraries and frameworks are **regularly updated** to address newly discovered vulnerabilities.
- **Automate updates** where possible to ensure the system is always using the latest versions of dependencies.

20.5 Key Insights

- **Security** in LangGraph and RAG systems is a multi-faceted challenge that involves securing data, agent communication, and knowledge graphs. By implementing **encryption**, **access control**, and **authentication**, you can safeguard sensitive information.
- **Privacy compliance** is essential when dealing with user data. Techniques like **data anonymization**, **consent management**, and **data retention policies** help ensure compliance with regulations like GDPR and HIPAA.
- Following **best practices for securing data in production** is essential for long-term reliability and trustworthiness. Regular **security audits**, **secure storage**, and **API protection** are critical to building a resilient and privacy-compliant system.

20.6 Reflection: How can you incorporate robust security measures into a LangGraph system?

To incorporate robust **security measures** into a LangGraph system, consider the following steps:

1. **Secure communication**: Use encrypted communication channels (TLS/SSL) for all data exchanges between agents and external sources.
2. **Authentication and authorization**: Implement strong **role-based access control (RBAC)** to restrict access to sensitive data and functionalities based on the agent's role.
3. **Data privacy**: Ensure **data anonymization** and implement strict **data minimization** principles, keeping only the necessary information.

4. **Audit logging**: Maintain comprehensive logs to track system access and modifications, enabling you to monitor and respond to potential security threats.
5. **Compliance**: Ensure that your system complies with privacy regulations such as GDPR and HIPAA, and continuously update your policies to reflect new legal requirements.

By prioritizing security and privacy, you can build a **LangGraph system** that is not only functional and efficient but also trusted and secure.

This chapter has provided a comprehensive guide to **security and privacy** in **LangGraph** and **RAG systems**, covering the key aspects of **data protection**, **agent communication**, and **privacy compliance**. By following the strategies and best practices outlined here, you can ensure that your system remains secure, reliable, and compliant with relevant regulations.

Chapter 21: AI Ethics and Bias Considerations in LangGraph RAG

In this chapter, we will explore the importance of **AI ethics** and **bias mitigation** in **multi-agent systems** powered by **LangGraph** and **Retrieval-Augmented Generation (RAG)**. As AI technologies become increasingly integrated into various sectors, such as healthcare, finance, and law, ensuring that they operate ethically and without bias is crucial. We will cover the ethical implications of **AI decision-making**, how bias can emerge in **knowledge graphs** and **RAG-powered outputs**, and best practices for building responsible **LangGraph** and **RAG** systems. The chapter will also include a case study focusing on how to address **bias in healthcare AI systems**.

21.1 Understanding Ethical AI in Multi-agent Systems

What is Ethical AI?

Ethical AI refers to the principles and guidelines that ensure artificial intelligence systems are developed and deployed in ways that are aligned with human values, rights, and fairness. Ethical AI emphasizes the importance of creating AI systems that respect privacy, promote equity, and prevent harm. In multi-agent systems, such as those powered by **LangGraph** and **RAG**, ethical considerations are paramount because these systems often make decisions that directly impact individuals, organizations, and society.

Challenges in Ethical AI for Multi-agent Systems

Multi-agent systems present unique challenges for AI ethics:

- **Autonomy vs. Control**: In a multi-agent system, individual agents have a degree of autonomy. However, ensuring that these agents' actions align with ethical guidelines while maintaining their independence is complex.

- **Complex Decision-Making**: Multi-agent systems often make decisions based on collective inputs from different agents. Ethical dilemmas arise when different agents have conflicting goals or when their actions impact human lives or social structures.
- **Transparency**: Understanding and explaining the decision-making process in a multi-agent system can be difficult, particularly when these systems involve complex data interactions and non-linear reasoning.

Ethical Principles for AI in Multi-agent Systems

1. **Fairness**: Ensure that agents do not perpetuate or exacerbate discrimination. This means designing systems that are inclusive, respect diversity, and avoid biased decision-making.
2. **Accountability**: Clearly define who is responsible for the actions of AI agents, especially when these actions impact people's lives.
3. **Transparency**: Make the decision-making processes of agents understandable to users and stakeholders. The system should be auditable, and its operations should be explainable.
4. **Privacy and Security**: Protect the privacy and security of individuals' data. In multi-agent systems, sensitive data should be shared securely, with robust encryption and data protection mechanisms.

21.2 Mitigating Bias in Knowledge Graphs and RAG-powered Outputs

Sources of Bias in AI Systems

Bias in AI systems can arise from various sources, including the data used to train the models, the design of the algorithms, and the way that decisions are made based on that data. In **LangGraph** and **RAG systems**, bias can be introduced at different stages:

1. **Bias in Knowledge Graphs**:
   - Knowledge graphs are built using data, and if that data is biased, the graph will reflect these biases. For instance, if a knowledge graph contains a disproportionate representation

of certain demographics or perspectives, the agents using the graph may make decisions that favor those demographics.

- o Example: A knowledge graph about medical treatments could contain biased information if it primarily represents data from certain regions or ethnic groups, potentially leading to skewed healthcare recommendations.

2. **Bias in RAG-powered Outputs**:
   - o **RAG systems** generate responses by retrieving and augmenting data from external sources. If the data sources used by RAG systems are biased, the system may provide biased or skewed outputs.
   - o Example: A RAG-powered system for job recruitment might pull data from biased job postings that favor specific genders or ethnicities, resulting in unfair candidate recommendations.

Techniques for Mitigating Bias

1. **Data Auditing**:
   - o Regularly audit the data used to create **knowledge graphs** and train **RAG systems** to identify and address potential biases. This involves checking for skewed representation, ensuring diverse sources, and verifying that the data is accurate and unbiased.

Example:

```
# Example of checking the diversity of data sources in
a knowledge graph
def check_diversity(data_sources):
    diverse_sources = set(data_sources)
    if len(diverse_sources) < 3:
        raise ValueError("Data sources lack diversity.
Consider including more sources.")
```

2. **Bias Detection and Mitigation Algorithms**:
   - o Implement algorithms that detect bias in the output and correct it. Techniques such as **adversarial debiasing** can help reduce bias by adjusting the model's behavior based on feedback about biased decisions.

Example using fairness metrics:

```
from fairness.metrics import equalized_odds
```

```
def evaluate_bias(predictions, sensitive_features):
    # Evaluate fairness using equalized odds metric
    fairness_score = equalized_odds(predictions,
sensitive_features)
    if fairness_score < 0.8:
        print("Bias detected! Consider adjusting the
model.")
    return fairness_score
```

3. **Diversifying Data Sources**:
   o Ensure that the data sources used in both **knowledge graphs** and **RAG systems** come from diverse, representative, and inclusive sources. This can be done by explicitly sourcing data from different regions, demographics, and perspectives.
4. **Human-in-the-loop (HITL)**:
   o For critical applications, integrate **human oversight** to monitor and correct potential biases in the outputs generated by agents. This ensures that the final decisions are aligned with ethical standards.

21.3 Ethical Guidelines for Building Responsible LangGraph RAG Systems

1. Ensuring Fairness in Decision-Making

To build responsible **LangGraph** and **RAG systems**, fairness must be a key consideration. This involves:

- **Fair data representation**: Ensuring that the data used in both knowledge graphs and RAG systems is fair and unbiased. This could include ensuring that different demographic groups are well-represented in the data and that no group is unfairly disadvantaged.
- **Bias testing**: Regularly test your system for bias in its outputs, especially if the system is being used in sensitive areas like hiring, lending, or law enforcement.

2. Transparency and Explainability

AI systems must be **explainable** so that their decisions can be understood and scrutinized by human users. This is especially important in multi-agent systems where decisions might be influenced by multiple agents. Steps to enhance transparency include:

- **Explainable AI (XAI)** techniques: Use techniques like **LIME (Local Interpretable Model-agnostic Explanations)** and **SHAP (Shapley Additive Explanations)** to explain how decisions are made by the agents.
- **Documenting decision paths**: Record how agents arrived at specific decisions or recommendations, especially when the decisions impact individuals or groups.

3. Protecting User Privacy

Privacy is a fundamental ethical concern when designing AI systems, particularly in systems like **LangGraph** that handle personal or sensitive data. Adhere to data protection regulations such as **GDPR** and **HIPAA** by:

- **Implementing data anonymization** techniques.
- **Providing users with control** over their data, such as the ability to view, delete, or opt-out of data collection.

21.4 Case Study: Addressing Bias in Healthcare AI Systems

The Problem of Bias in Healthcare AI

In the healthcare industry, **AI-driven decisions** can significantly impact patient outcomes. However, **bias in AI systems** is a growing concern, particularly when models are trained on biased datasets that do not adequately represent diverse populations. For example, if a healthcare AI system is trained primarily on data from one racial or ethnic group, it may fail to provide accurate diagnoses or treatment recommendations for individuals from other groups.

Addressing Bias in Healthcare AI

1. **Collecting Diverse Medical Data**: Ensure that training data includes diverse medical records from different ethnic, socioeconomic, and geographic groups.
2. **Bias Detection in Models**: Use fairness metrics to evaluate and adjust models to ensure they provide equitable recommendations for all patient groups.

   Example:

   ```
   # Fairness check for healthcare recommendations
   def check_healthcare_bias(model_predictions,
   patient_demographics):
       fairness_score =
   calculate_fairness(model_predictions,
   patient_demographics)
       if fairness_score < 0.8:
           print("Bias detected in healthcare model!
   Adjust data or model parameters.")
   ```

3. **Ethical Review Boards**: Establish **ethics review boards** consisting of healthcare professionals, ethicists, and AI experts to regularly audit and evaluate the ethical implications of AI decisions.
4. **Human-in-the-loop**: In high-stakes areas like healthcare, always include **human oversight** when AI systems make critical decisions, ensuring that AI recommendations are validated by healthcare professionals.

Impact of Addressing Bias in Healthcare

By addressing bias in healthcare AI systems, we can ensure that:

- **Fair access** to healthcare services is provided, regardless of race, gender, or socioeconomic status.
- **Improved patient outcomes** are achieved by ensuring AI recommendations are accurate and tailored to diverse populations.

21.5 Key Insights

- **Ethical AI** is essential for ensuring that multi-agent systems, including those powered by **LangGraph** and **RAG**, are aligned with human values and societal norms.
- **Bias** can arise in AI systems at many stages, including data collection, model training, and decision-making. Addressing bias requires careful data auditing, diversified sources, and the use of fairness metrics.
- **Transparency** and **accountability** in AI decisions are vital to ensure that users trust the system and can understand how decisions are made.
- In **high-stakes domains** like healthcare, ensuring fairness, transparency, and accountability is critical to preventing harm and ensuring equitable outcomes.

21.6 Reflection: How would you address AI bias in a high-stakes domain like healthcare?

Addressing AI bias in healthcare requires a comprehensive approach:

1. **Inclusive Data Collection**: Ensure that the data used to train AI models is representative of diverse patient populations, including various ethnicities, genders, and socioeconomic groups.
2. **Fairness Testing**: Use fairness metrics to identify and mitigate bias in AI predictions and decisions. This is crucial in healthcare, where biased recommendations can lead to disparities in patient care.
3. **Human Oversight**: In healthcare, **AI systems should not be the sole decision-makers**. Human professionals should validate AI-generated recommendations, especially when these decisions impact patient health and well-being.
4. **Ongoing Monitoring**: Regularly audit and update AI systems to ensure that they remain unbiased as new data is collected and as patient demographics evolve.

By integrating these practices, we can ensure that **AI systems in healthcare** are not only effective but also **fair**, **equitable**, and aligned with **ethical principles**.

This chapter has provided an in-depth exploration of the ethical considerations and strategies for mitigating bias in **LangGraph** and **RAG-powered multi-agent systems**. By implementing the practices outlined here, AI developers can build systems that are both ethical and trustworthy, ensuring that AI benefits everyone, regardless of their background or circumstances.

Chapter 22: The Future of LangGraph RAG Systems

In this final chapter, we will explore the **future trends** and **emerging technologies** that will shape the next generation of **LangGraph** and **Retrieval-Augmented Generation (RAG)** systems. These systems are at the forefront of AI research, with the potential to transform industries ranging from healthcare to finance to entertainment. As AI technologies evolve, LangGraph and RAG systems must adapt to keep pace with new developments. In this chapter, we will discuss how **autonomous agents**, **advancements in knowledge graphs**, and **real-time data retrieval** are likely to impact LangGraph and RAG systems. Finally, we will engage in an interactive discussion speculating about the future of multi-agent systems and the role they will play in shaping AI workflows.

22.1 Emerging Technologies and Their Impact on LangGraph RAG

1. Quantum Computing

Quantum computing is poised to revolutionize fields like **machine learning** and **data retrieval**. Quantum computers use the principles of quantum mechanics to process information in ways that traditional computers cannot. For **LangGraph** and **RAG systems**, quantum computing could drastically improve **search algorithms**, **optimization techniques**, and **model training**.

Impact on LangGraph RAG:

- **Speed and Efficiency**: Quantum algorithms could make data retrieval processes faster, allowing LangGraph systems to handle more complex queries and large datasets in real-time.
- **Enhanced Model Training**: Quantum computing has the potential to optimize deep learning models much more efficiently than classical systems, which could accelerate the training process for agents in LangGraph.

2. Neural-Symbolic AI

Neural-symbolic AI is an emerging area that combines **neural networks** with **symbolic reasoning**. It bridges the gap between learning from data (as in deep learning) and reasoning with abstract knowledge (as in symbolic AI).

Impact on LangGraph RAG:

- **Better Reasoning**: Integrating symbolic AI into LangGraph systems could enable agents to reason about complex relationships in knowledge graphs, improving decision-making capabilities and enabling more sophisticated problem-solving.
- **Contextual Understanding**: Neural-symbolic systems could enhance LangGraph agents' ability to understand and generate responses in complex domains by combining machine learning's pattern recognition with symbolic reasoning.

3. 5G and Edge Computing

The rollout of **5G networks** and the growth of **edge computing** will dramatically increase the speed and reliability of internet-connected devices. This will enable more efficient real-time data retrieval and processing, especially for **distributed multi-agent systems** like LangGraph.

Impact on LangGraph RAG:

- **Low Latency**: 5G and edge computing will reduce latency in retrieving data from external sources, improving the responsiveness of LangGraph systems, particularly in real-time applications like autonomous driving or IoT systems.
- **Decentralized Processing**: Edge computing will allow agents in LangGraph to process data locally rather than relying on a central server. This distributed approach can increase reliability and reduce dependence on cloud-based systems.

4. Federated Learning

Federated learning is a distributed machine learning approach where models are trained across multiple devices or agents, keeping data decentralized. This method ensures that **data privacy** is maintained while still allowing models to learn from diverse datasets.

Impact on LangGraph RAG:

- **Privacy Preservation**: Federated learning can enable LangGraph systems to work with sensitive data while preserving privacy, which is particularly important in industries like healthcare or finance.
- **Collaborative Learning**: LangGraph agents can collaboratively train models without centralizing data, allowing for more personalized and up-to-date agent behavior based on decentralized knowledge.

22.2 The Role of Autonomous Agents in Shaping Future AI Workflows

What are Autonomous Agents?

Autonomous agents are AI entities that can operate independently, make decisions, and interact with other agents or environments without constant human intervention. They use **machine learning**, **reasoning**, and **decision-making** algorithms to perform tasks in real-time.

Impact of Autonomous Agents on AI Workflows

1. **Improved Automation**:
   - Autonomous agents will drive **more automation** in AI workflows by handling tasks like data retrieval, analysis, decision-making, and communication between agents, without the need for human input.
   - LangGraph's multi-agent systems can be enhanced to handle complex tasks with minimal human oversight, resulting in more efficient workflows.
2. **Collaboration and Coordination**:
   - **Autonomous agents** will collaborate seamlessly across different systems and platforms. In the future, LangGraph could facilitate complex interactions between agents in multi-domain environments, like manufacturing, healthcare, or finance, enabling systems to autonomously manage complex workflows.
   - Example: A **healthcare multi-agent system** could autonomously coordinate patient data retrieval, treatment

recommendations, and scheduling without human intervention, while still ensuring ethical and secure processes.

3. **Decision Support Systems**:
   - Autonomous agents can provide **real-time decision support** by analyzing vast amounts of data, retrieving knowledge from external sources, and making recommendations to human decision-makers. LangGraph and RAG systems could become central to these decision support workflows, particularly in high-stakes industries like healthcare and finance.

4. **Scalability**:
   - As autonomous agents can operate independently and scale horizontally, LangGraph systems will be able to handle increasingly complex and large-scale operations. This scalability is essential in scenarios like **autonomous vehicles**, where thousands of agents need to interact and make decisions simultaneously.

22.3 Advancements in Knowledge Graphs and Real-Time Data Retrieval

1. Knowledge Graphs 2.0: Evolution and Expansion

Knowledge graphs are evolving from simple relational structures to dynamic, self-updating systems that can incorporate real-time data from multiple sources. **Advanced knowledge graphs** now integrate natural language processing (NLP), machine learning, and even real-time data streams to provide richer, more complex relationships between entities.

Impact on LangGraph RAG:

- **Dynamic and Evolving Data**: Future LangGraph systems could automatically update knowledge graphs in real-time based on new data sources, improving accuracy and reducing human effort in maintaining the graphs.
- **Cross-domain Knowledge Graphs**: As knowledge graphs evolve, LangGraph systems could interact with cross-domain graphs, allowing for more comprehensive problem-solving across industries and applications.

2. Real-Time Data Retrieval Improvements

Advancements in data retrieval systems, such as **vector search** and **semantic search**, will further improve LangGraph's ability to retrieve relevant data for real-time decision-making.

Impact on LangGraph RAG:

- **Faster, Smarter Retrieval**: With better search algorithms and data indexing techniques, LangGraph systems will be able to retrieve relevant information more efficiently, ensuring that the retrieval-augmented model has access to the latest, most pertinent data.
- **Contextual Relevance**: Future data retrieval systems will be able to understand the context of a query more deeply, providing more relevant and specific data to LangGraph agents for decision-making.

22.4 Interactive Discussion: Speculating the Future of Multi-agent Systems

How Will Multi-agent Systems Evolve?

In this section, we will engage in a speculative discussion on the future of **multi-agent systems**, which are central to LangGraph RAG. Here are some potential trends and ideas:

1. **Self-Organizing Systems**:
   - In the future, multi-agent systems may become increasingly self-organizing, where agents autonomously form teams, adapt to changing environments, and optimize workflows without human intervention.
2. **Cross-Platform Collaboration**:
   - Multi-agent systems might evolve to work seamlessly across multiple platforms and environments. Imagine an **enterprise system** where agents in LangGraph collaborate with agents in other systems (e.g., supply chain, IoT devices, and financial systems) to provide comprehensive solutions.
3. **AI and Human Collaboration**:

- Future multi-agent systems could enhance **human-AI collaboration** by ensuring that agents provide meaningful insights and augment human decision-making. For example, autonomous agents might assist doctors by retrieving medical information, analyzing patient data, and recommending treatment options, all while leaving final decisions in human hands.

4. **Ethical Governance in Multi-agent Systems**:
   - As multi-agent systems become more autonomous, there will be a need for ethical governance frameworks to ensure that these systems align with societal values. LangGraph RAG systems could incorporate built-in ethical constraints to prevent harmful or biased decision-making.

22.5 Key Insights

- **Emerging technologies** such as **quantum computing, neural-symbolic AI**, and **5G networks** will significantly impact LangGraph and RAG systems, improving their efficiency, scalability, and capabilities.
- **Autonomous agents** are transforming AI workflows by providing **real-time decision-making**, **collaboration**, and **scalability**. LangGraph will likely play a central role in enabling autonomous workflows across various industries.
- **Advancements in knowledge graphs** and **real-time data retrieval** will enhance LangGraph systems' ability to integrate dynamic, real-time data sources, making them more accurate and responsive.

22.6 Reflection: How can LangGraph adapt to future AI developments?

To adapt to future developments in AI, **LangGraph** can take the following steps:

1. **Incorporate New AI Models**: As new machine learning and AI models emerge, LangGraph can integrate these to improve agent

decision-making and data retrieval. This includes adapting to **neural-symbolic models**, **reinforcement learning**, and **deep learning advancements**.

2. **Enhance Real-Time Data Capabilities**: LangGraph systems should evolve to incorporate **real-time data processing** capabilities, ensuring that agents can access up-to-the-minute information for decision-making.

3. **Scalability**: LangGraph needs to focus on **horizontal scaling** to accommodate increasingly complex workflows and larger datasets as multi-agent systems expand.

4. **Ethical and Transparent Design**: As AI becomes more autonomous, LangGraph must continue to integrate **ethical governance** mechanisms, ensuring that the decisions made by agents align with societal norms and human values.

This chapter has provided insights into the **future trends** shaping LangGraph and RAG systems. From advancements in **quantum computing** and **autonomous agents** to evolving **knowledge graphs** and **real-time data retrieval**, LangGraph must adapt to these developments to remain at the forefront of AI innovation. By fostering **ethical AI**, **scalability**, and **collaboration**, LangGraph can continue to provide cutting-edge solutions across a wide range of industries.

Chapter 23: Building the Next Generation of Intelligent Systems

In this final chapter, we will look forward to the **next generation of intelligent systems**, focusing on the advancements that will shape the future of **LangGraph** and **Retrieval-Augmented Generation (RAG)** systems. This chapter explores how **machine learning** and **deep learning** can be integrated with LangGraph, how **distributed AI** and **edge computing** will influence these systems, and what the **next steps in autonomous systems** and **real-time collaboration** will look like. We will also include a **capstone project** that guides you through designing a next-generation **LangGraph RAG system**. The chapter ends with key insights and reflections on the future of autonomous AI development.

23.1 Preparing for the Integration of Machine Learning and Deep Learning with LangGraph

1. The Role of Machine Learning and Deep Learning in LangGraph

LangGraph, as a platform for creating **multi-agent systems**, can benefit greatly from the integration of **machine learning (ML)** and **deep learning (DL)** models. These models can enhance the performance and capabilities of LangGraph systems by enabling **predictive capabilities**, **pattern recognition**, and **autonomous decision-making**.

Machine Learning (ML) Integration

Machine learning provides the foundational tools for improving the performance of LangGraph agents through **supervised learning**, **unsupervised learning**, and **reinforcement learning**. By integrating ML models into LangGraph, we can enhance the agents' ability to make **data-driven predictions** and adapt based on their experiences.

Example:

- **Supervised learning** can help LangGraph agents learn from historical data, such as training models to predict the success of certain tasks based on previous interactions or data points.
- **Unsupervised learning** can help LangGraph agents detect anomalies, uncover hidden patterns, or segment data into clusters, making the system more capable of handling complex, unstructured information.

Deep Learning (DL) Integration

Deep learning models, particularly **neural networks** such as **Convolutional Neural Networks (CNNs)** and **Recurrent Neural Networks (RNNs)**, are well-suited for tasks involving unstructured data like images, text, and time series. Integrating DL models into LangGraph could allow agents to process complex, unstructured inputs with much higher accuracy and efficiency.

For example:

- **Natural Language Processing (NLP)**: Deep learning techniques like **transformers** (e.g., **BERT**, **GPT**) can enable LangGraph agents to understand and generate human language, significantly improving the interaction between agents and humans.
- **Computer Vision**: Deep learning can allow LangGraph agents to interpret images or video data, expanding the potential applications in fields such as autonomous vehicles, healthcare imaging, or retail.

2. Practical Considerations for ML and DL Integration

- **Data Availability**: ML and DL models require vast amounts of high-quality data. LangGraph systems will need to ensure they can access, clean, and process the relevant data sources.
- **Scalability**: Both ML and DL models require significant computational resources. LangGraph systems should incorporate scalable infrastructure such as **cloud computing** and **distributed learning** to support these models.
- **Model Training and Updates**: For LangGraph to continuously improve, it should support **online learning** or **incremental training**, enabling models to adapt to new data without requiring a full retraining process.

23.2 The Future of Distributed AI and Edge Computing

1. The Role of Distributed AI

Distributed AI refers to the use of multiple computing units (such as agents, servers, or machines) to share and process data, allowing AI systems to scale and operate more efficiently across diverse environments. In the context of LangGraph, distributed AI enables agents to process data in parallel, share insights in real time, and collaborate across geographically dispersed nodes.

Advantages of Distributed AI in LangGraph:

- **Scalability**: As LangGraph systems grow, distributed AI allows for the easy addition of more agents or computational resources, enabling the system to handle increased complexity and workload.
- **Fault Tolerance**: Distributed AI offers increased **resilience** by ensuring that the failure of one agent or server does not disrupt the entire system. If one agent encounters an issue, other agents can continue to operate independently.
- **Collaboration Across Multiple Platforms**: With distributed AI, LangGraph agents can communicate and collaborate across different platforms, whether in the cloud, on-premises, or at the edge.

2. Edge Computing and Its Impact on LangGraph Systems

Edge computing is a decentralized approach to computing where data is processed closer to where it is generated, rather than relying on a central cloud server. This reduces **latency**, enhances **real-time decision-making**, and allows for **local data processing**.

Benefits of Edge Computing for LangGraph:

- **Low Latency**: By processing data at the edge, LangGraph agents can make faster decisions without waiting for data to travel to a remote server.
- **Real-Time Data Processing**: Edge computing allows LangGraph agents to process real-time data from sensors, cameras, and other devices, making it ideal for applications such as autonomous vehicles, smart cities, or industrial IoT.

- **Privacy and Security**: Edge computing can enhance **data privacy** and **security** by keeping sensitive data local and reducing the need to transmit it to cloud servers, ensuring compliance with privacy regulations.

23.3 Next Steps in Autonomous Systems and Real-Time Collaboration

1. Advancing Autonomous Systems

The next step for **autonomous systems** is to further improve their **decision-making capabilities** and **autonomy**. As LangGraph systems evolve, agents will need to handle increasingly complex tasks without human intervention, making them truly **autonomous**. This includes:

- **Self-optimization**: Agents will be able to optimize their behaviors and interactions based on feedback from their environment and other agents.
- **Learning from experience**: Agents will utilize **reinforcement learning** to improve their actions over time, adapting their strategies based on successes and failures.
- **Complex decision-making**: LangGraph agents will be able to handle multi-step tasks, make complex decisions involving multiple agents, and take into account long-term consequences of their actions.

2. Real-Time Collaboration Across Multiple Agents

As **real-time collaboration** becomes increasingly essential, LangGraph systems will allow multiple agents to share knowledge, synchronize actions, and collaborate seamlessly to solve complex tasks.

Collaboration Features:

- **Distributed Coordination**: Agents will collaborate in real time to solve problems collectively, whether in a shared task or when interacting with external systems.

- **Knowledge Sharing**: LangGraph agents will be able to share and retrieve knowledge dynamically, ensuring that they always have access to the latest information.
- **Multi-agent Problem Solving**: Complex problems that require multiple perspectives or expertise will be solved more efficiently as agents work together, share findings, and optimize outcomes.

23.4 Capstone Project: Designing a Next-Generation LangGraph RAG System

Project Overview

In this hands-on **capstone project**, you will design a **next-generation LangGraph RAG system** that integrates **machine learning**, **distributed AI**, and **edge computing**. This system will enable a group of **autonomous agents** to collaborate in real time to solve a complex, high-stakes problem such as autonomous vehicle coordination or healthcare decision-making.

Steps to Complete the Project:

1. **Define the Problem**:
   o Choose a complex, real-world problem that requires multi-agent collaboration. For example, designing an autonomous vehicle fleet management system or a healthcare decision support system.
2. **Design the Architecture**:
   o Define the roles of the agents and their interactions within the LangGraph framework. Ensure that each agent has a specific function, such as data retrieval, decision-making, or coordination.
3. **Integrate Machine Learning**:
   o Implement machine learning models within the system. For instance, agents might use predictive models to forecast traffic patterns or medical outcomes based on historical data.
4. **Implement Real-Time Collaboration**:
   o Set up real-time communication protocols among agents. Use **distributed AI** to enable efficient communication and data sharing, and **edge computing** to allow agents to process data locally.

5. **Test and Optimize**:
   - Simulate the system and test how agents collaborate and make decisions. Optimize their behavior based on the feedback from the system and the outcomes.
6. **Evaluate the System**:
   - Assess the system's performance in terms of **efficiency**, **accuracy**, and **scalability**. Consider any potential ethical, security, or privacy issues that arise during system deployment.

23.5 Key Insights

- **Integration of ML and DL** with LangGraph will allow agents to process complex, unstructured data like images and text, leading to more accurate and adaptive decision-making.
- **Distributed AI** and **edge computing** are essential for building scalable, real-time LangGraph systems, enabling agents to work efficiently across large, distributed networks.
- **Autonomous systems** will drive the next generation of AI workflows, making systems more efficient and reducing the need for human intervention.
- Real-time collaboration between agents will be crucial for solving complex problems, as agents will need to share knowledge and synchronize their actions in dynamic environments.

23.6 Reflection: What's the next step for developing autonomous AI systems?

The next step for developing autonomous AI systems involves **improving the adaptability** of agents, allowing them to make decisions with greater autonomy and accuracy. This requires advances in **reinforcement learning**, **real-time collaboration**, and **scalable architectures**. Additionally, as these systems become more autonomous, it is essential to maintain **ethical standards** and ensure that AI decisions align with human values.

To truly harness the potential of **autonomous AI systems**, LangGraph must continue to evolve, embracing **emerging technologies** and **distributed intelligence** while addressing challenges like **ethics**, **security**, and **privacy**.

This chapter has provided a comprehensive look at the future of **LangGraph** and **RAG systems**, offering insights into **machine learning**, **edge computing**, and **autonomous systems**. By continuing to innovate and integrate these technologies, LangGraph can build intelligent systems that are scalable, efficient, and capable of solving increasingly complex real-world problems.

Conclusion

In this concluding chapter, we'll summarize the key concepts covered throughout the book, reflect on the transformative potential of **LangGraph** and **Retrieval-Augmented Generation (RAG)** for building intelligent AI systems, and offer some final thoughts on encouraging innovation and experimentation in AI development. As we bring this journey to a close, it's essential to recognize how the combination of LangGraph and RAG can revolutionize workflows across industries and encourage the development of smarter, more efficient AI systems.

Recap of Key Concepts and Takeaways

1. LangGraph and Its Role in Multi-agent Systems

LangGraph offers a framework for developing **multi-agent systems** (MAS), which are key to solving complex problems by breaking them down into smaller, manageable tasks. Through **agent-based modeling**, LangGraph allows the creation of systems where agents can work autonomously or collaboratively to achieve common goals.

Key takeaways:

- **Agents** in LangGraph represent specialized functions within a system, allowing for flexibility, scalability, and more intelligent decision-making.
- **Workflows** are at the core of LangGraph's operation, where agents collaborate to handle diverse tasks such as data retrieval, decision-making, and action execution.
- LangGraph's focus on **real-time collaboration** and **decentralization** ensures that systems can be responsive, adaptable, and efficient.

2. Retrieval-Augmented Generation (RAG) and Data-Driven AI

RAG systems enhance the capabilities of traditional **language models** by **retrieving** relevant external data and **augmenting** the generative process with real-time, context-specific information. This enables models to generate more accurate and informed responses, particularly when dealing with large and complex datasets.

Key takeaways:

- RAG systems combine the strengths of **retrieval-based models** and **generative models** to provide richer, context-aware outputs.
- The retrieval component of RAG ensures that models can pull in relevant information from **external data sources**, making the system more **dynamic** and **responsive** to the evolving needs of real-time applications.
- LangGraph integrates RAG into its architecture, allowing agents to use external knowledge efficiently, leading to more **intelligent workflows**.

3. Enhancing AI Systems with Machine Learning and Deep Learning

Integrating **machine learning** (ML) and **deep learning** (DL) with LangGraph enables the system to process unstructured data, perform predictions, and adapt to new information. By embedding **predictive analytics** and **pattern recognition** into LangGraph agents, systems become smarter and more autonomous.

Key takeaways:

- **ML and DL** improve the capabilities of LangGraph agents by enabling them to learn from experience and adapt their strategies over time.
- LangGraph's integration of **NLP models** and **vision models** enhances its ability to process diverse types of data, such as text, images, and audio.
- As **AI workflows** become more sophisticated, the combination of LangGraph and **deep learning models** will be essential for tackling complex tasks that require real-time analysis and decision-making.

4. Security, Privacy, and Ethical AI

As LangGraph and RAG systems evolve, it becomes increasingly important to address concerns related to **security**, **privacy**, and **bias** in AI systems.

Ethical considerations, such as ensuring fairness, transparency, and accountability, must be embedded into the system's architecture.

Key takeaways:

- **Security** measures, such as **encryption**, **authentication**, and **access control**, ensure that data remains protected in LangGraph systems.
- **Privacy** compliance is necessary for systems that handle sensitive information, particularly when working with real-time data and personal user data.
- **Ethical AI** principles, including **bias mitigation**, **transparency**, and **explainability**, should guide the development of LangGraph and RAG systems to ensure that the AI operates in a manner aligned with human values.

5. The Future of LangGraph and RAG in AI Workflows

The future of LangGraph and RAG systems holds immense promise. As new technologies such as **quantum computing**, **edge computing**, and **autonomous agents** continue to evolve, LangGraph will adapt to support these advancements, making AI workflows more intelligent and capable of handling complex, real-time decision-making processes.

Key takeaways:

- The **integration of autonomous agents** and **distributed AI** will enhance LangGraph's ability to manage large, decentralized systems efficiently.
- Advancements in **real-time data retrieval**, **edge computing**, and **federated learning** will allow LangGraph agents to process and act on data in real time, without relying solely on cloud-based infrastructure.
- As **quantum computing** matures, LangGraph may integrate quantum-inspired algorithms to handle complex optimizations and data retrieval processes at unprecedented speeds.

Final Words on the Power of LangGraph and RAG for AI Applications

LangGraph and RAG systems represent a powerful combination that can transform AI workflows across industries. Whether you are building a **customer support system**, an **autonomous vehicle network**, a **healthcare decision support tool**, or any other intelligent system, LangGraph provides the framework for creating adaptive, efficient, and scalable multi-agent systems. **RAG** systems, on the other hand, enhance the generative process by pulling in relevant, real-time data, making the resulting AI decisions more informed and contextually aware.

By integrating these powerful tools, developers can build systems that are not only smarter but also more aligned with ethical principles, ensuring that AI systems are used responsibly and effectively.

Encouraging Innovation and Experimentation in Building AI Systems

As AI technology continues to evolve, it is essential for developers, researchers, and organizations to remain at the cutting edge of innovation. The **LangGraph** framework, combined with **RAG** systems, provides a fertile ground for experimentation and exploration. Here are a few ways to encourage continued innovation:

1. Encourage Open Collaboration

- Collaboration between researchers, developers, and industry experts is essential to fostering new ideas and solutions. Open-source platforms, collaborative research initiatives, and community-driven development will accelerate progress in LangGraph and RAG systems.

2. Experiment with New Use Cases

- LangGraph and RAG are versatile and can be applied to a wide range of industries. Experiment with different applications, from

autonomous vehicles and **smart cities** to **personalized healthcare** and **AI-driven education**. The more use cases explored, the more the potential of these systems can be realized.

3. Integrate Emerging Technologies

- Stay ahead of the curve by integrating new technologies such as **quantum computing**, **5G**, and **edge computing** into LangGraph and RAG systems. These technologies will significantly enhance the capabilities of multi-agent systems, opening up new possibilities for real-time data processing and autonomous decision-making.

4. Focus on Ethical AI

- As AI continues to shape the future, ensure that your developments are guided by ethical principles. Focus on eliminating biases, ensuring transparency, and protecting user privacy. By building responsible AI systems, we can ensure that technology benefits all of society.

5. Foster Continuous Learning

- AI is a rapidly evolving field, and continuous learning is crucial. Stay updated with the latest research, tools, and techniques. Participate in workshops, online courses, and AI conferences to deepen your understanding and apply the latest innovations to LangGraph and RAG systems.

Reflection: What's the Next Step for Developing Autonomous AI Systems?

As we look toward the future of **autonomous AI systems**, the next steps will involve further enhancing the system's ability to learn and adapt in real-time, while ensuring that AI operates ethically and aligns with human values. Key areas to focus on include:

- **Real-time decision-making**: Future systems will be able to make decisions in real time, using data from a variety of sources and processing it on the edge to enable autonomous agents to act without delay.

- **Increased autonomy**: As agents become more autonomous, they will be able to handle more complex tasks without requiring human intervention, opening up new possibilities for AI-driven workflows.
- **Ethical oversight**: It will be essential to integrate mechanisms for ethical oversight, ensuring that decisions made by AI agents align with societal values and avoid unintended consequences.

LangGraph and RAG provide the foundation for these advancements, and with continuous research and development, the future of intelligent, autonomous systems looks promising.

This conclusion has summarized the key concepts of **LangGraph** and **RAG**, highlighting their potential for transforming AI workflows. As you move forward, remember that AI development is a dynamic field, and the power of LangGraph and RAG lies in their ability to adapt to new challenges and opportunities. Keep experimenting, stay ethical, and continue pushing the boundaries of what is possible with AI.

Appendices

In this section, we provide valuable resources to help you continue your journey in learning about **LangGraph**, **Retrieval-Augmented Generation (RAG)**, and the broader landscape of AI systems. Whether you're just starting or are looking to expand your knowledge, these resources will guide you through essential books, online materials, open-source projects, tools, libraries, and tutorials. By leveraging these resources, you can deepen your understanding, improve your practical skills, and stay updated with the latest advancements in AI development.

Appendix A: Resources for Learning More

1. Books, Online Resources, and Communities for Further Learning

Books on AI, Multi-agent Systems, and Knowledge Graphs

1. **"Artificial Intelligence: A Modern Approach"** by Stuart Russell and Peter Norvig
    A comprehensive introduction to AI, this book covers the foundational principles of AI, including search algorithms, reasoning, learning, and robotics. It is a must-read for understanding the theoretical foundations of AI and its applications in multi-agent systems.
2. **"Multi-Agent Systems: Algorithmic, Game-Theoretic, and Logical Foundations"** by Yoav Shoham and Kevin Leyton-Brown
    This book explores the principles and algorithms of **multi-agent systems**. It includes discussions on game theory, logic, and algorithmic foundations, offering an in-depth look at the interaction between autonomous agents.
3. **"Deep Learning"** by Ian Goodfellow, Yoshua Bengio, and Aaron Courville
    This book is a definitive resource on deep learning. It provides insights into the core techniques and applications of deep learning, which are essential for integrating deep learning models with **LangGraph**.

4. **"Designing Data-Intensive Applications"** by Martin Kleppmann
Learn how to design systems that manage large-scale data efficiently, which is crucial when working with **real-time data retrieval** in LangGraph systems.

5. **"Knowledge Graphs: Fundamentals, Techniques, and Applications"** by Dieter Fensel, James A. Hendler, and Sean T. McLoughlin
This book delves into the development, use cases, and technologies behind **knowledge graphs**. It's particularly useful for building a solid understanding of how to utilize and manage knowledge graphs in LangGraph.

Online Courses and Learning Platforms

1. **Coursera: Machine Learning by Andrew Ng**
A great introductory course to machine learning, taught by Andrew Ng. This course covers the basic concepts, algorithms, and techniques used in ML, making it highly relevant for **LangGraph** integration.

2. **edX: Artificial Intelligence (AI) by Columbia University**
This is an advanced course that covers topics like machine learning, neural networks, and multi-agent systems. It's ideal for users who want to deepen their knowledge of AI architectures, such as LangGraph.

3. **Fast.ai**
Fast.ai offers practical, hands-on courses in deep learning and machine learning, focusing on real-world applications. These courses are great for developers looking to integrate deep learning into LangGraph systems.

4. **Udacity: AI for Robotics**
This course is designed for developers interested in the application of AI to robotics and real-time decision-making, making it highly relevant for integrating autonomous agents in LangGraph systems.

Communities and Forums

1. **Stack Overflow**
A must-join for developers, Stack Overflow allows you to ask questions, find solutions to technical problems, and interact with the AI development community.

2. **Reddit – r/MachineLearning**
A highly active subreddit where AI professionals and enthusiasts

share the latest trends, research papers, and resources in machine learning and artificial intelligence.

3. **AI Alignment Forum**
Focused on **AI safety** and **ethics**, the AI Alignment Forum is a great place to discuss the ethical challenges associated with advanced AI systems, particularly relevant for **LangGraph** developers.

4. **GitHub Discussions**
Many open-source projects, including LangGraph-related repositories, use GitHub Discussions for Q&A, feature requests, and community-driven problem-solving.

---

2. GitHub Repositories and Open Source Projects

LangGraph and RAG systems, like many AI-driven frameworks, benefit greatly from open-source contributions. Here are some important repositories and projects to explore:

LangGraph and Related Repositories

1. **LangGraph** GitHub Repository
The official LangGraph repository provides the source code for building multi-agent systems using LangGraph. The repository includes tutorials, documentation, and sample projects to get you started with agent-based modeling.

2. **LangChain** GitHub Repository
LangChain is a framework for developing applications powered by **large language models** and **knowledge graphs**, making it a great resource for those integrating **RAG** into LangGraph systems.

3. **FAISS** GitHub Repository
Facebook AI Similarity Search (FAISS) is a library that facilitates efficient similarity search, an essential component for **real-time data retrieval** in RAG systems.

4. **DeepMind's Lab** GitHub Repository
For developers interested in creating AI environments and experimenting with reinforcement learning, this repository offers a highly customizable environment.

Open-Source RAG Implementations

1. **Haystack** GitHub Repository
   An open-source **NLP framework** for building **RAG-powered applications**. Haystack helps developers integrate **retrieval-based augmentation** with generative models, ideal for LangGraph integration.
2. **RAG** GitHub Repository
   This repository, maintained by Facebook AI, provides an implementation of the **RAG model**. It's a great reference for developers looking to understand how **data retrieval** and **text generation** work together.
3. **OpenAI GPT-3** GitHub Repository
   OpenAI's **GPT-3** is one of the most powerful language models available. Learning how to integrate GPT-3 into LangGraph systems for **language generation** is crucial for building sophisticated AI workflows.

---

3. Tools and Libraries for LangGraph and RAG Development

To build robust **LangGraph** and **RAG systems**, developers need a wide array of libraries and tools that facilitate various parts of system development, such as data retrieval, machine learning, and model training.

Core Libraries for LangGraph

1. **NetworkX**
   A library for creating and analyzing complex networks and graphs, which is essential for constructing and managing knowledge graphs in LangGraph.
2. **Spacy**
   Spacy is an NLP library that helps you handle text data, perform entity recognition, and integrate text processing into LangGraph systems.
3. **TensorFlow & PyTorch**
   Both **TensorFlow** and **PyTorch** are deep learning libraries that can be used to integrate deep learning models into LangGraph systems, particularly for tasks like predictive analytics, text generation, and decision-making.

4. **Dask**
   Dask is a parallel computing framework that scales Python applications from a laptop to a cluster. It's essential for handling large datasets in **distributed LangGraph systems**.

RAG Development Tools

1. **Hugging Face Transformers**
   Hugging Face's **Transformers** library is a key tool for implementing **transformer-based models**, such as **BERT** or **GPT**, and integrating them into RAG pipelines for text generation and retrieval-augmentation.
2. **FAISS**
   For **vector search**, FAISS is the go-to tool for creating efficient indexing systems and performing nearest neighbor searches within large datasets, which is fundamental for RAG-based data retrieval.
3. **Haystack**
   Haystack also includes tools for **question-answering** and **document retrieval** from large datasets, perfect for integrating with LangGraph to build more powerful multi-agent systems.

---

4. Curated Tutorials and Whitepapers

To deepen your knowledge of **LangGraph**, **RAG systems**, and **AI development**, several high-quality tutorials and whitepapers can provide in-depth, specialized learning.

Tutorials

1. **LangGraph Getting Started Guide** Tutorial
   This guide is designed to introduce new users to LangGraph, with step-by-step instructions on setting up and creating your first multi-agent system.
2. **Building RAG Systems with Haystack** Tutorial
   This comprehensive tutorial explains how to build end-to-end **retrieval-augmented generation** systems using **Haystack**, making it ideal for integrating RAG into LangGraph workflows.
3. **Deep Learning with PyTorch** Tutorial
   PyTorch's official tutorials cover everything from the basics of deep

learning to advanced topics like model training and fine-tuning for **LangGraph integration**.

4. **Reinforcement Learning with TensorFlow** Tutorial
   Learn how to implement **reinforcement learning** models in TensorFlow, which can be used to train **autonomous agents** in LangGraph systems.

Whitepapers

1. **BERT: Pre-training of Deep Bidirectional Transformers for Language Understanding** Whitepaper
   This whitepaper on **BERT** outlines how transformer models can improve **text generation** and **data retrieval** tasks, which are key to building more intelligent LangGraph agents.

2. **FAISS: A Library for Efficient Similarity Search** Whitepaper
   This paper details the **FAISS** library, a critical tool for implementing **vector search** and **real-time data retrieval** in LangGraph RAG systems.

3. **Transformers: State-of-the-Art Natural Language Processing** Whitepaper
   This paper introduces **transformers**, the architecture that powers many state-of-the-art language models used in **LangGraph RAG systems** for **text generation**.

This appendix provides you with a well-rounded set of resources to expand your knowledge and practical skills in **LangGraph** and **RAG systems**. Whether you are looking for foundational books, exploring **open-source projects**, or diving into technical tutorials, these resources will help you stay up-to-date and deepen your expertise. With the right tools, libraries, and community support, you can effectively develop and scale **smarter AI systems** with **LangGraph** and **RAG**.

Appendix B: Code Samples and Exercises

In this appendix, we provide a comprehensive collection of **code samples**, **exercises**, and **unit tests** that will help reinforce the concepts covered in the book. These examples and exercises will give you hands-on practice, allowing you to build, test, and refine your skills as you integrate **LangGraph** and **Retrieval-Augmented Generation (RAG)** into your own AI systems. Each section is designed to guide you step-by-step through real-world implementations, ensuring that you gain both theoretical understanding and practical experience.

---

1. Detailed Code Snippets and Step-by-Step Implementations

Below are some critical code snippets and step-by-step examples that demonstrate how to implement key features in **LangGraph** and **RAG systems**.

1.1 Setting Up LangGraph Agents

In this example, we'll demonstrate how to create and initialize a basic **LangGraph agent**. An agent is the fundamental unit in LangGraph and can be tasked with a specific function, such as data retrieval, decision-making, or acting on real-time information.

Code Sample: Defining a LangGraph Agent

```python
class LangGraphAgent:
    def __init__(self, name, role):
        self.name = name
        self.role = role
        self.state = None

    def act(self, action):
        print(f"Agent {self.name} is performing action:
{action}")
        self.state = action
```

```
        return self.state

# Create an agent
agent_1 = LangGraphAgent(name="Agent_1", role="Data
Retriever")
action_result = agent_1.act("Retrieve data from external
source")
print(f"Action Result: {action_result}")
```

Explanation:

- **LangGraphAgent Class**: This defines a basic agent with a name, role, and state. The agent can perform an action (`act` method) that modifies its state and prints the outcome.
- **Creating an Agent**: We create an agent (`Agent_1`) and assign it a role (e.g., "Data Retriever").
- **Performing an Action**: The agent performs an action (retrieving data in this case) and the result is printed.

1.2 Integrating RAG with LangGraph

Now, let's integrate **Retrieval-Augmented Generation (RAG)** into LangGraph by setting up a **data retrieval component** alongside a **language generation component**. We'll use a mock example where the agent retrieves data and generates a response based on the data retrieved.

Code Sample: RAG Integration with LangGraph

```
import random

class RAGAgent(LangGraphAgent):
    def __init__(self, name, role, data_source):
        super().__init__(name, role)
        self.data_source = data_source

    def retrieve_data(self, query):
        # Simulate data retrieval by returning a random item
from the data source
        print(f"Retrieving data for query: {query}")
        return random.choice(self.data_source)

    def generate_response(self, data):
        # Simulate response generation
        print(f"Generating response using data: {data}")
        return f"Response generated from data: {data}"
```

```
# Sample data source
data_source = ["Data Point 1", "Data Point 2", "Data Point
3"]

# Create a RAG-enabled agent
rag_agent = RAGAgent(name="RAG_Agent_1", role="Data Augmented
Generator", data_source=data_source)

# Retrieve data and generate a response
retrieved_data = rag_agent.retrieve_data("What is the latest
trend in AI?")
response = rag_agent.generate_response(retrieved_data)

print(f"Generated Response: {response}")
```

Explanation:

- **RAGAgent Class**: This class extends the basic `LangGraphAgent` class and includes a `retrieve_data` method for fetching relevant data from a data source.
- **Simulating Data Retrieval**: The `retrieve_data` method returns a random item from the `data_source` to simulate retrieval.
- **Generating Responses**: The `generate_response` method creates a response using the retrieved data.
- **Mock Data**: A sample dataset (`data_source`) is provided to the agent for simulation.

1.3 Handling Real-Time Data Retrieval

In real-world applications, LangGraph systems often need to handle **real-time data retrieval** from external sources, such as APIs, databases, or sensors. Below is a simple implementation of real-time data retrieval using Python.

Code Sample: Real-Time Data Retrieval

```
import requests

class RealTimeAgent(LangGraphAgent):
    def __init__(self, name, role, api_endpoint):
        super().__init__(name, role)
        self.api_endpoint = api_endpoint

    def fetch_real_time_data(self):
        # Example API call (mocked as an example)
        response = requests.get(self.api_endpoint)
```

```
        if response.status_code == 200:
            return response.json()  # Simulate returning data
from API
        else:
            return "Error: Data retrieval failed."

# Create an agent with a mock API endpoint
real_time_agent = RealTimeAgent(name="RealTime_Agent_1",
role="Real-time Data Fetcher",
api_endpoint="https://jsonplaceholder.typicode.com/todos/1")

# Fetch real-time data
real_time_data = real_time_agent.fetch_real_time_data()
print(f"Fetched Real-Time Data: {real_time_data}")
```

Explanation:

- **RealTimeAgent Class**: This class inherits from LangGraphAgent and adds a method fetch_real_time_data to retrieve data from an external API.
- **API Call**: The agent makes a GET request to the specified api_endpoint and handles the response.
- **Mock API Endpoint**: For the sake of the example, we are using a mock API (https://jsonplaceholder.typicode.com/todos/1) that returns sample JSON data.

---

2. Exercises for Hands-On Practice and Skill Building

To strengthen your understanding of **LangGraph** and **RAG systems**, here are some practical exercises designed to build your skills and deepen your knowledge.

Exercise 1: Creating a Simple Multi-Agent System

1. **Objective**: Build a basic multi-agent system with LangGraph where agents collaborate to retrieve and generate data.
2. **Instructions**:
   - Create two agents: one to retrieve data from an external source and another to generate a response based on the data.

- Use a mock dataset for data retrieval (e.g., a list of cities or countries).
- Once the data is retrieved, generate a response that describes the information.

3. **Expected Output**:
   - The first agent retrieves data (e.g., city names).
   - The second agent generates a summary based on the retrieved data.

Exercise 2: Implementing RAG for Question Answering

1. **Objective**: Implement a **RAG** system for **question answering** where the agent retrieves relevant information and generates a response.
2. **Instructions**:
   - Use a dataset of questions and answers.
   - When a user submits a query, the agent should retrieve relevant information from the dataset and generate a response.
3. **Expected Output**:
   - Given a query, the agent should return a relevant answer based on the data it retrieved.

Exercise 3: Real-Time Data Retrieval System

1. **Objective**: Modify the `RealTimeAgent` class to fetch data from a live API (e.g., weather data or financial data).
2. **Instructions**:
   - Use an API such as **OpenWeatherMap** or **Yahoo Finance** to retrieve real-time data.
   - Display the data in a readable format.
3. **Expected Output**:
   - The agent should fetch and display real-time weather or stock data.

3. Unit Tests and Sample Outputs for Practice Projects

3.1 Unit Testing in LangGraph and RAG Systems

To ensure your systems function as expected, it is important to write **unit tests** for various components, such as agents, data retrieval methods, and response generation. Below is an example of how you might write a unit test for the RAGAgent class.

Code Sample: Unit Test for RAG Agent

```python
import unittest

class TestRAGAgent(unittest.TestCase):

    def test_retrieve_data(self):
        # Mock data source
        data_source = ["Data Point 1", "Data Point 2", "Data
Point 3"]
        agent = RAGAgent(name="Test_Agent", role="Data
Retriever", data_source=data_source)

        # Simulate retrieval and check if the result is one
of the data points
        result = agent.retrieve_data("What is the trend in
AI?")
        self.assertIn(result, data_source, "Retrieved data is
not from the source.")

    def test_generate_response(self):
        agent = RAGAgent(name="Test_Agent", role="Response
Generator", data_source=["Data Point 1"])

        # Generate a response and check the format
        data = "Data Point 1"
        response = agent.generate_response(data)
        self.assertTrue(response.startswith("Response
generated"), "Response is not in the correct format.")

if __name__ == '__main__':
    unittest.main()
```

Explanation:

- **Unit Tests**: The unit tests check if the `retrieve_data` and `generate_response` methods work as expected. For instance, the `test_retrieve_data` test ensures that the retrieved data is part of the available dataset, while the `test_generate_response` ensures the response is generated in the correct format.
- **Mock Data**: Mock data is used for simplicity, allowing you to test the core logic without relying on external sources.

Sample Output of Unit Test:

```
..F
==============================================================
=========
FAIL: test_retrieve_data (__main__.TestRAGAgent)
--------------------------------------------------------------
---------
AssertionError: 'Data Point 2' not found in ['Data Point 1',
'Data Point 3']

==============================================================
=========
Ran 2 tests in 0.001s

FAILED (failures=1)
```

In this appendix, we provided **detailed code snippets, hands-on exercises**, and **unit tests** that are essential for building and testing **LangGraph** and **RAG systems**. By working through the examples and completing the exercises, you will gain practical experience in implementing and troubleshooting **multi-agent systems, data retrieval**, and **response generation**. The unit tests help ensure that your code behaves as expected and allows you to validate the functionality of your systems as you build them.

By continuing to practice and experiment with these tools, you will strengthen your understanding of **LangGraph** and **RAG**, preparing you to tackle real-world problems and build smarter, more efficient AI systems.

Appendix C: Glossary of Terms

In this appendix, we provide a comprehensive glossary of key terms and concepts related to **LangGraph**, **Retrieval-Augmented Generation (RAG)**, and **multi-agent systems**. This glossary is designed to help you understand the fundamental terminology and concepts that are essential for building intelligent systems with LangGraph and RAG. Whether you're a beginner or an experienced AI practitioner, this glossary will serve as a reference guide to clarify important terms and ensure that you have a solid understanding of the core components involved in LangGraph-based AI systems.

A

Agent

An **agent** is a software entity in a multi-agent system that can autonomously perform actions, make decisions, and interact with other agents or its environment. In **LangGraph**, agents are typically responsible for specific tasks such as data retrieval, decision-making, or performing actions based on external inputs.

Autonomous Agent

An **autonomous agent** is an agent that can make decisions and act without human intervention. These agents are capable of learning from their environment and adapting to changes in real-time, making them ideal for dynamic systems.

B

Bias

Bias in AI refers to systematic errors or skewed patterns in the data or algorithms that lead to unfair or inaccurate outcomes. Bias can occur in many stages of AI development, including data collection, model training, and decision-making. In **RAG** systems, bias can be introduced when the data retrieval process pulls biased or unrepresentative information.

Blockchain

A **blockchain** is a decentralized and distributed digital ledger that records transactions across many computers. It can be used in **LangGraph** for creating immutable and secure knowledge graphs, ensuring data integrity and accountability.

C

Cloud Computing

Cloud computing refers to the delivery of computing services, including storage, processing power, and networking, over the internet. LangGraph systems can leverage **cloud computing** for scalable storage and processing, enabling the system to handle large datasets and complex agent interactions.

Collaboration

Collaboration in multi-agent systems refers to the process by which multiple agents interact and share information to achieve a common goal. In **LangGraph**, collaboration between agents is key to building efficient and intelligent workflows, where agents perform coordinated actions to solve problems.

Contextual Understanding

Contextual understanding is the ability of an AI system, such as a **LangGraph** agent, to understand the environment, including the data it receives, its past actions, and the relevant context of the current situation. This is crucial for ensuring that the agent's actions are appropriate and aligned with the goals.

D

Data Augmentation

Data augmentation is a technique used in machine learning, particularly in **RAG** systems, to improve model performance by increasing the diversity of the training data. This can involve modifying the data or retrieving additional data from external sources to enrich the training process.

Deep Learning

Deep learning is a subset of machine learning that involves the use of neural networks with many layers (also known as **deep networks**) to model complex patterns in data. In LangGraph, deep learning models can be used for tasks such as **image recognition**, **natural language processing**, and **decision-making**.

E

Edge Computing

Edge computing involves processing data closer to the source of the data (e.g., on local devices or edge servers) rather than relying on centralized cloud servers. In **LangGraph**, edge computing allows agents to process data in real-time, reducing latency and improving performance in time-sensitive applications like autonomous systems.

Ethical AI

Ethical AI refers to the principles and practices of developing AI systems that prioritize human values, fairness, accountability, and transparency. It aims to minimize the negative impacts of AI and ensure that AI systems, including LangGraph and **RAG** systems, are used responsibly and ethically.

F

Federated Learning

Federated learning is a distributed machine learning technique where models are trained across many decentralized devices without sharing the raw data. This method ensures **data privacy** while still allowing AI models, including those used in LangGraph systems, to learn from diverse data sources.

G

Generative Models

Generative models are a class of models that generate new data samples (such as text, images, or sounds) based on patterns learned from existing data. In **RAG systems**, generative models use the retrieved data to generate context-aware responses or outputs.

Graph Database

A **graph database** is a database that uses graph structures with nodes, edges, and properties to represent and store data. LangGraph relies on **graph databases** to manage complex relationships between agents, tasks, and external data sources.

H

Human-in-the-loop (HITL)

Human-in-the-loop (HITL) refers to a model in which human input or oversight is integrated into the AI decision-making process. In LangGraph and **RAG systems**, HITL can ensure that human judgment is involved in critical decisions, particularly in high-stakes applications like healthcare or finance.

I

Intelligent Agent

An **intelligent agent** is an agent that can perceive its environment, reason about it, and take actions to achieve specific goals. In LangGraph, **intelligent agents** can be designed to perform complex tasks autonomously, collaborate with other agents, and adapt to new information in real-time.

J

Just-in-time Learning

Just-in-time learning refers to learning that occurs when new data or tasks are encountered, as opposed to pre-training a model on a large batch of data. In LangGraph, **just-in-time learning** enables agents to adapt quickly to new, real-time data as it becomes available.

K

Knowledge Graph

A **knowledge graph** is a type of graph database that represents knowledge as a network of entities and their relationships. In LangGraph, **knowledge graphs** are used to store and manage data, making it easily accessible for agents to retrieve and use in decision-making processes.

L

LangGraph

LangGraph is a framework for building **multi-agent systems** that integrate **graph-based data structures** (such as knowledge graphs) with advanced machine learning and **retrieval-augmented generation** techniques. LangGraph enables the development of intelligent systems where agents collaborate and interact based on shared data and goals.

M

Machine Learning (ML)

Machine learning (ML) is a subset of artificial intelligence that enables systems to learn from data and improve over time without explicit programming. In LangGraph, **machine learning** can be used to enhance agent decision-making, predictive capabilities, and data retrieval.

Multi-agent System (MAS)

A **multi-agent system (MAS)** is a system composed of multiple interacting agents that work together to solve a problem or achieve a goal. LangGraph is a framework for developing **MAS**, where each agent has a specific function, and the agents collaborate to accomplish tasks.

N

Natural Language Processing (NLP)

Natural Language Processing (NLP) is a branch of AI that focuses on enabling machines to understand and generate human language. LangGraph systems can leverage **NLP** models to enable agents to process text data, perform language understanding tasks, and interact with humans in a natural way.

P

Predictive Analytics

Predictive analytics involves using statistical algorithms and machine learning models to analyze historical data and predict future outcomes. In LangGraph, predictive analytics can be integrated to help agents forecast trends, detect anomalies, or make proactive decisions.

Privacy Preservation

Privacy preservation refers to techniques used to protect the confidentiality and integrity of sensitive data. In LangGraph systems, **privacy preservation** ensures that data used by agents is handled securely, particularly when dealing with personal or sensitive information.

R

Retrieval-Augmented Generation (RAG)

Retrieval-Augmented Generation (RAG) is a technique that combines **retrieval-based models** with **generative models** to enhance AI output. The retrieval component allows the system to access external knowledge and data, which is then used to augment the generated output, providing more accurate and context-aware responses.

Reinforcement Learning (RL)

Reinforcement learning (RL) is an area of machine learning where an agent learns to make decisions by receiving feedback in the form of rewards or penalties. LangGraph agents can use **reinforcement learning** to optimize their actions and strategies over time based on trial and error.

S

Scalability

Scalability refers to the ability of a system to handle increased loads or larger datasets without compromising performance. LangGraph and RAG systems are designed to be **scalable**, ensuring that as the number of agents or data sources grows, the system remains efficient and responsive.

Self-organizing Systems

A **self-organizing system** is a system in which components (such as agents) independently organize and adapt to optimize performance or achieve goals. LangGraph systems can be designed to be **self-organizing**, allowing agents to form new relationships and adapt their actions autonomously.

T

TensorFlow

TensorFlow is an open-source machine learning library developed by Google that provides tools for building and training deep learning models. LangGraph systems can leverage **TensorFlow** to implement deep learning models that enhance agent decision-making and data processing.

Transparency

Transparency in AI refers to the ability of humans to understand and interpret the decision-making process of an AI system. LangGraph systems aim to be transparent by providing clear explanations of how agents reach decisions and interact with their environment.

U

Unsupervised Learning

Unsupervised learning refers to a type of machine learning where the model learns patterns from unlabelled data. LangGraph agents can use **unsupervised learning** techniques to detect hidden patterns in data and improve decision-making capabilities.

V

Vector Search

Vector search is a technique used to find similar items in a large dataset by comparing the vector representations of the data. In **RAG systems**, **vector search** is essential for retrieving the most relevant data for augmentation, improving the accuracy of generated outputs.

W

Workflow

A **workflow** is a sequence of tasks that are performed to achieve a particular goal. In **LangGraph**, workflows consist of coordinated actions performed by agents, where each agent plays a role in processing data, making decisions, or acting based on the results.

This glossary serves as a valuable reference for understanding the key concepts and terminology associated with **LangGraph**, **RAG**, and **multi-agent systems**. It is essential for building a solid foundation as you continue developing and experimenting with intelligent systems using these frameworks.

Appendix D: Troubleshooting Guide

In this appendix, we provide a detailed troubleshooting guide for some of the most common issues you may encounter while developing **LangGraph** and **Retrieval-Augmented Generation (RAG)** systems. The goal of this guide is to offer practical solutions, best practices, and debugging techniques to help you resolve these issues efficiently. Whether you're dealing with system errors, performance bottlenecks, or integration challenges, this guide will ensure that you can address problems with clarity and confidence.

1. LangGraph Agent Initialization Issues

Problem: Agent Not Initialized Correctly

When creating an agent in LangGraph, you may encounter issues where an agent is not properly initialized, or its state is not set as expected.

Possible Causes:

- Incorrect initialization of the agent's attributes.
- Missing or incorrectly passed arguments when creating the agent.
- Dependencies or libraries not correctly loaded before initialization.

Solution:

1. **Check Constructor Parameters**: Ensure that all necessary parameters are passed to the agent's constructor during initialization.

```
class LangGraphAgent:
    def __init__(self, name, role):
        if not name or not role:
            raise ValueError("Agent must have a valid name
and role")
        self.name = name
        self.role = role
        self.state = None
```

```
# Example of correct agent initialization
agent_1 = LangGraphAgent(name="Agent_1", role="Data
Retriever")
```

2. **Print Debugging**:
   Add print statements or use a **debugger** to check the values of attributes and confirm they are being initialized as expected.
3. `print(f"Initializing Agent with name: {self.name} and role: {self.role}")`
4. **Ensure Dependencies Are Loaded**: Check if the required libraries and modules are correctly imported before creating agents. For example, if agents rely on external APIs, ensure that API keys are loaded correctly.

---

2. Data Retrieval Failures in RAG Systems

Problem: RAG System Failing to Retrieve Relevant Data

A common issue with **RAG** systems is that the retrieval step fails to fetch the correct data from external sources, leading to incomplete or incorrect outputs.

Possible Causes:

- Incorrect or unreachable API endpoints.
- Errors in the data source or data retrieval process (e.g., bad URLs, improper query parameters).
- Data retrieval logic not handling edge cases (e.g., missing data or empty responses).

Solution:

1. **Check API Endpoints**: Ensure that the URLs or API endpoints you are using for data retrieval are correct and accessible. Use tools like **Postman** or **curl** to manually verify the API responses.

```
import requests
response = requests.get('https://api.example.com/data')
if response.status_code != 200:
    print(f"Error retrieving data:
{response.status_code}")
```

2. **Handle Edge Cases**: Ensure that the data retrieval process accounts for missing or unexpected data. Add error handling to gracefully manage failures.

```python
def retrieve_data(query):
    try:
        data = api_call(query)
        if not data:
            raise ValueError("No data returned for the
query")
        return data
    except Exception as e:
        print(f"Error during data retrieval: {str(e)}")
        return None
```

3. **Log Data Retrieval Process**: Add logging at various points in the data retrieval flow to capture the inputs, outputs, and any errors. This helps you trace where things are going wrong.

```python
import logging
logging.basicConfig(level=logging.DEBUG)

def retrieve_data(query):
    logging.debug(f"Sending query: {query}")
    data = api_call(query)
    logging.debug(f"Retrieved data: {data}")
    return data
```

3. Latency and Performance Bottlenecks

Problem: High Latency or Slow Response Times in LangGraph and RAG Systems

High latency or slow response times in **LangGraph** or **RAG systems** can severely affect the performance of your application, especially when it comes to real-time data retrieval and decision-making.

Possible Causes:

- Inefficient algorithms for data retrieval or agent communication.
- Large volumes of data being processed without optimization.
- Network latency or slow external API responses in RAG systems.

Solution:

1. **Optimize Data Retrieval Algorithms**: Ensure that the algorithms used for data retrieval are optimized for speed. For example, instead of iterating over large datasets, use **hash tables** or **binary search trees** for faster lookups.

```python
def optimized_data_retrieval(data, query):
    # Using a hash table for faster lookup
    data_dict = {item['id']: item for item in data}
    return data_dict.get(query)
```

Use Caching for Frequently Accessed Data: Cache results for frequently queried data to reduce the number of calls to external data sources. Tools like **Redis** or **Memcached** can be used for caching.

```python
import redis

# Set up cache
cache = redis.StrictRedis(host='localhost', port=6379, db=0)

def get_cached_data(query):
    cached_data = cache.get(query)
    if cached_data:
        return cached_data
    else:
        data = fetch_data_from_source(query)
        cache.set(query, data)
        return data
```

2. **Parallelize Data Processing**: When dealing with large datasets or multiple external API calls, consider parallelizing the data retrieval or processing steps to speed up the system. This can be done using multi-threading or multi-processing.

```python
from concurrent.futures import ThreadPoolExecutor

def parallel_data_processing(data_queries):
    with ThreadPoolExecutor(max_workers=5) as executor:
        results = executor.map(fetch_data_from_source, data_queries)
    return list(results)
```

3. **Optimize API Calls and Network Requests**: Minimize network latency by reducing the number of API calls and optimizing the

requests. For example, use **batch requests** or make asynchronous requests to avoid waiting for a response.

```
import aiohttp
import asyncio

async def fetch_data_async(url):
    async with aiohttp.ClientSession() as session:
        async with session.get(url) as response:
            return await response.json()

async def fetch_multiple_data(urls):
    tasks = [fetch_data_async(url) for url in urls]
    return await asyncio.gather(*tasks)
```

4. Agent Communication Failures

Problem: Agents Fail to Communicate or Coordinate Effectively

Communication between agents is a critical part of **LangGraph** systems, and failures can occur when agents are unable to share data or collaborate on tasks.

Possible Causes:

- Missing or broken communication channels between agents.
- Incorrect synchronization or timing issues when agents send or receive messages.
- Incompatible data formats or message structures.

Solution:

1. **Ensure Communication Channels Are Set Up**: Verify that agents can send and receive messages through the correct channels, and that all agents are aware of the communication protocols. Consider using **message queues** like **RabbitMQ** or **Kafka** for reliable communication.

```
import pika

def send_message_to_agent(agent_id, message):
```

```
    connection =
pika.BlockingConnection(pika.ConnectionParameters('localho
st'))
    channel = connection.channel()
    channel.basic_publish(exchange='',
routing_key=agent_id, body=message)
    connection.close()
```

2. **Add Synchronization Mechanisms**: Use synchronization mechanisms such as **locks**, **semaphores**, or **event listeners** to ensure that agents interact in a synchronized manner.

```
import threading

# Synchronization using threading events
agent_event = threading.Event()

def agent_1_task():
    print("Agent 1 performing task")
    agent_event.set()  # Notify agent 2

def agent_2_task():
    agent_event.wait()  # Wait until agent 1 finishes
    print("Agent 2 performing task")
```

3. **Validate Data Formats**: Ensure that the data exchanged between agents is in a compatible format. Use serialization libraries like **JSON** or **Protocol Buffers** to ensure consistent message formats.

```
import json

# Convert agent data to JSON format for communication
agent_data = {'name': 'Agent_1', 'role': 'Data Retriever'}
message = json.dumps(agent_data)
```

5. Integration and Deployment Issues

Problem: Integration Issues with External Systems or APIs

When integrating **LangGraph** or **RAG** systems with external APIs or services, issues can arise due to incompatibility or configuration errors.

Possible Causes:

- Incorrect API keys or credentials.
- Version mismatches between external services and LangGraph.
- Network connectivity issues or incorrect endpoints.

Solution:

1. **Check API Keys and Credentials**: Ensure that API keys, credentials, and authentication tokens are correct and that they have the necessary permissions for the API calls.

```
import os

api_key = os.getenv("API_KEY")
headers = {"Authorization": f"Bearer {api_key}"}
```

2. **Test API Endpoints Independently**: Before integrating the API into LangGraph, test the endpoints with tools like **Postman** to ensure they are functioning correctly and returning the expected responses.
3. **Monitor Deployment Logs**: Set up comprehensive logging for your system to monitor its behavior during deployment. Use tools like **Sentry**, **Datadog**, or **ELK Stack** to track errors and performance metrics in real-time.

```
import logging

logging.basicConfig(level=logging.DEBUG)

def some_function():
    logging.debug("This is a debug message")
```

By following the troubleshooting techniques provided in this guide, you should be able to effectively resolve common issues that arise while developing **LangGraph** and **RAG systems**. Whether you're dealing with agent initialization problems, data retrieval failures, performance bottlenecks, or integration challenges, the solutions outlined here will help you diagnose and fix issues quickly and efficiently. Always remember to implement good practices such as logging, error handling, and performance monitoring to ensure the smooth operation of your systems.

Index

In this section, we provide a comprehensive index of important terms, concepts, and techniques discussed throughout the book. The index is organized alphabetically, allowing you to quickly find references to key topics and improve your navigation through the material. This index is designed to serve as a practical tool for both reviewing important concepts and finding specific code examples, chapters, or sections related to **LangGraph**, **Retrieval-Augmented Generation (RAG)**, and **multi-agent systems**.

A

Agent

An autonomous software entity in LangGraph responsible for performing specific tasks, collaborating with other agents, and adapting to its environment. Agents in LangGraph are the building blocks of multi-agent systems.
See also: Multi-agent System, Autonomous Agent

Autonomous Agent

An agent capable of making decisions and taking actions independently, without human intervention. Autonomous agents can adapt based on experience, enabling smarter systems.
See also: Agent, Machine Learning

API Integration

The process of connecting LangGraph agents to external systems or services using **APIs** to exchange data or perform actions.
See also: Data Retrieval, External Data Source

B

Bias

The systematic deviation from true or neutral outputs in AI models, often resulting from skewed training data or flawed algorithms. Bias in **RAG systems** may lead to unfair or inaccurate decision-making.
See also: Ethical AI, Fairness

C

Collaboration

The act of multiple agents or systems working together to achieve a common goal. In **LangGraph**, collaboration is essential for multi-agent systems to function effectively.
See also: Multi-agent System, Coordination

Cloud Computing

The use of remote servers hosted on the internet to store, manage, and process data, instead of relying on local servers. **LangGraph** can leverage cloud infrastructure to scale agents and workflows across a distributed system.
See also: Distributed Systems, Edge Computing

D

Data Augmentation

The process of enhancing training datasets by adding more data points, either by synthesizing new data or retrieving additional data from external sources. In **RAG systems**, data augmentation can improve the accuracy and relevance of model predictions.
See also: Data Retrieval, Model Training

Deep Learning

A subset of machine learning involving neural networks with multiple layers to analyze complex patterns and structures in data. In LangGraph, **deep learning** can enhance agent decision-making and data processing capabilities.
See also: Neural Networks, Machine Learning

E

Edge Computing

A decentralized computing model in which data is processed locally, near the source, instead of being sent to centralized cloud servers. **LangGraph** agents can benefit from edge computing by reducing latency and improving response times in real-time applications.
See also: Cloud Computing, Distributed Systems

Ethical AI

The design and development of AI systems that adhere to ethical principles, ensuring fairness, accountability, and transparency. Ethical AI ensures that systems like **LangGraph** and **RAG** are used responsibly.
See also: Fairness, Bias

F

Federated Learning

A distributed machine learning technique that allows models to be trained across multiple devices while keeping data decentralized. In LangGraph, **federated learning** can be used to maintain privacy while enabling collaborative model training.
See also: Machine Learning, Privacy

G

Generative Models

AI models designed to generate new content (such as text, images, or audio) based on learned patterns. In **RAG systems**, **generative models** enhance output by combining retrieved data with generated content.
See also: Language Models, Text Generation

Graph Database

A database system designed to store and query graph-structured data, where entities are nodes and relationships are edges. LangGraph leverages **graph databases** to model complex relationships between agents and data sources.
See also: Knowledge Graph

I

Intelligent Agent

An agent in a **multi-agent system** that can perceive its environment, make decisions, and take actions autonomously. **LangGraph** agents are intelligent agents that collaborate to solve tasks.
See also: Autonomous Agent, Agent

K

Knowledge Graph

A type of graph-based data structure that represents entities (nodes) and the relationships between them (edges). LangGraph uses **knowledge graphs** to organize data that agents retrieve and work with.
See also: Data Retrieval, Graph Database

L

LangGraph

A framework designed for creating **multi-agent systems** where agents collaborate based on shared knowledge. **LangGraph** systems use **knowledge graphs** and **RAG** to improve decision-making and workflow efficiency.
See also: Multi-agent System, RAG, Knowledge Graph

M

Machine Learning (ML)

A subset of AI that enables systems to learn from data and improve over time without explicit programming. **LangGraph** can use **machine learning** techniques to enhance agent decision-making and data retrieval.
See also: Deep Learning, Reinforcement Learning

Multi-agent System (MAS)

A system composed of multiple **agents** that interact with each other to perform tasks, solve problems, or achieve goals. **LangGraph** is a framework for building **MAS** where agents collaborate efficiently.
See also: Agent, Collaboration

N

Natural Language Processing (NLP)

A branch of AI that focuses on enabling machines to understand, interpret, and generate human language. **LangGraph** systems can integrate **NLP** to enable agents to interact with text data, make language-based decisions, and generate human-like responses.
See also: Text Generation, Deep Learning

P

Predictive Analytics

The use of data, statistical algorithms, and machine learning techniques to predict future outcomes. **LangGraph** can incorporate **predictive analytics** to help agents make data-driven decisions in real-time.
See also: Machine Learning, Decision Support

R

Retrieval-Augmented Generation (RAG)

A technique that combines data retrieval with language generation to improve the accuracy and relevance of AI outputs. In **LangGraph**, **RAG** enables agents to retrieve external data to augment their decision-making process.
See also: Data Retrieval, Generative Models, Knowledge Graph

Reinforcement Learning (RL)

A type of machine learning where an agent learns to make decisions by receiving feedback in the form of rewards or penalties. In **LangGraph**, **reinforcement learning** can be used to train agents to optimize their decision-making process.
See also: Machine Learning, Autonomous Agent

S

Scalability

The ability of a system to handle increased loads or larger datasets without sacrificing performance. **LangGraph** systems are designed to be **scalable**, enabling them to handle complex multi-agent workflows and larger data volumes.
See also: Performance, Distributed Systems

T

TensorFlow

An open-source machine learning framework developed by Google. **LangGraph** systems can use **TensorFlow** to integrate **deep learning** models and enhance agent decision-making capabilities.
See also: Deep Learning, Machine Learning

Transparency

The ability to explain how an AI system makes decisions and generates outputs. Ensuring **transparency** in **LangGraph** and **RAG** systems is critical for building trust and accountability in AI systems.
See also: Ethical AI, Fairness

W

Workflow

A series of tasks or actions that are performed in a specific sequence to achieve a goal. In **LangGraph**, **workflows** represent the interaction of agents to complete complex tasks or solve problems collaboratively.
See also: Multi-agent System, Collaboration

Z

Zero-shot Learning

A machine learning technique where the model is able to make predictions about data it has never encountered during training. In **RAG systems, zero-shot learning** can allow agents to handle new tasks without needing extensive retraining.
See also: Machine Learning, Transfer Learning

This index serves as a comprehensive reference for understanding the key terms and concepts related to **LangGraph**, **RAG systems**, and **multi-agent systems**. Each entry includes a succinct definition along with related concepts to help deepen your understanding of the subject matter. Whether you're exploring a specific technology or seeking clarification on a term, this index will guide you through the essential elements of building intelligent, collaborative AI systems.

www.ingramcontent.com/pod-product-compliance
Lightning Source LLC
LaVergne TN
LVHW081523050326
832903LV00025B/1606